Building Interoperable Web Services

WS-I Basic Profile 1.0

patterns & practices

Andrew Mason, Microsoft Corporation
Jonathan Wanagel, Microsoft Corporation
Sandy Khaund, Microsoft Corporation
Sharon Smith, Microsoft Corporation
RoAnn Corbisier, Microsoft Corporation
Chris Sfanos, Microsoft Corporation

ISBN 0-7356-1844-5

Contents

1

Introduction

Building Interoperable Web Service: WS-I Basic Profile 1.0 is intended to help software architects and developers design and code Web services that are interoperable. We emphasize "interoperable" because we assume that you already understand how to implement a Web service. Our goal is to show you how to ensure that your Web service will work across multiple platforms and programming languages and with other Web services. Our philosophy is that you can best achieve interoperability by adhering to the guidelines set forth by the Web Services Interoperability (WS-I) organization in their Basic Profile version 1.0. In this book, we will show you how to write Web services that conform to those guidelines. Focusing on interoperability means there are some Web service issues that fall outside the scope of the discussion. These issues include security, performance optimization, scalability, and bandwidth conservation.

Note: For information on developing Web services, see the "More Information" section in this chapter.

How to Use this Book

This book is divided into five chapters. Here is a brief description of what each chapter contains.

Chapter 1, Introduction

This chapter discusses the WS-I. It includes the following topics:

- Why the WS-I was formed
- The organizational structure of the WS-I
- The problems the WS-I addresses, and those it does not
- The deliverables the WS-I provides

Chapter 2, The WS-I Deliverables

To encourage interoperability, the WS-I is creating a series of profiles, which will define how the underlying components of any Web service must work together. Chapter 2 discusses the first of these profiles, called the Basic Profile, and includes the following topics:

- The Basic Profile's underlying principles
- An explanation of the WS-I usage scenarios
- An explanation of the WS-I sample application, which demonstrates how to write a compliant Web service
- An explanation of the testing tools, which check that your implementation follows the Basic Profile guidelines

Chapter 3, How to Apply the Basic Profile

This chapter lists some general practices you should follow for writing Web services or clients that conform to Basic Profile.

Chapter 4, Applying Basic Profile Rules When Implementing Web Services

This chapter assigns each of the profile's rules to one of four possible levels of compliancy and, on a rule-by-rule basis, shows how to adjust your code to make your Web service comply with the profile's rules.

Chapter 5, Applying Basic Profile Rules When Consuming Web Services

This chapter assigns each of the profile's rules to one of four possible levels of compliancy and, on a rule-by-rule basis, shows how to adjust your code to make your Web service client comply with the profile's rules.

Appendix A

Appendix A groups the Basic Profile's rules according to their level of compliancy for implementing a Web service.

Appendix B

Appendix B groups the Basic Profile's rules according to their level of compliancy for implementing a Web service client.

Documentation Conventions

This guide uses the style conventions and terminology shown in Table 1.1.

Table 1.1 Document Conventions

Element	Meaning
bold font	Characters that you type exactly as shown, including commands and switches. Programming elements, such as methods, functions, data types, and data structures appear in bold font (except when part of a code sample, in which case they appear in monospace font). User interface elements are also bold.
Italic font	Variables for which you supply a specific value. For example, *Filename.ext* could refer to any valid file name for the case in question. New terminology also appears in italic on first use.
`Monospace font`	Code samples.
%SystemRoot%	The folder in which Windows is installed.

The Impetus Behind the WS-I

Simply put, Web services are programs that expose services to clients. However, unlike other distributed computing systems that include their own communications protocol, Web services are, as their name implies, adapted to the Web, and use Web-based standards. Web services, in essence, make the Internet a programming library available to developers worldwide.

Software and hardware vendors alike are rushing Web services products to market. The widespread adoption of core standards, such as XML, SOAP, WSDL, and UDDI, represents a significant breakthrough in the industry. Applications can now be built using a combination of components from multiple suppliers. However, for Web services to truly fulfill their promise, they must be interoperable. An interoperable Web service is one that works across platforms, applications, and languages as well as with Web services from other vendors.

Interoperability requires consensus, a clear understanding of requirements, and adherence to specifications. In response to these needs, industry members formed the WS-I, whose goals are to:

- Provide education and guidance that will further the adoption of Web services
- Promote consistent and reliable practices that will help developers write Web services that are interoperable across platforms, applications, and programming languages
- Articulate and promote a common industry vision for Web services interoperability to ensure that Web services evolve in a systematic, coherent fashion

To achieve its goals, the WS-I employs a variety of strategies, including:

- Implementation and testing guidance
- Web services profiles

Implementation guidance advises developers on the best practices for using such primary Web service components as XML, SOAP, WSDL, and UDDI. Testing guidance is available in the form of test tools that verify if a Web service adheres to the conformance guidelines set forth by the WS-I.

Web service profiles collect key Web service specifications into meaningful groups and simplify the implementation of interoperable applications. By demonstrating how each of these standards relates to the others, profiles also promote the adoption of those standards. The WS-I plans to constantly improve the scope and definition of the profiles to reflect the growing maturity of the underlying standards and the demands of the market.

Note that the WS-I is not itself a standards body. Rather, it cooperates with other industry groups and acts as a point of integration for the standards they generate.

The WS-I maintains a web site at *http://www.ws-i.org/*.

Members of the WS-I include software vendors, enterprise customers, and anyone interested in promoting interoperable Web services. Members vote to approve the adoption and distribution of any materials developed by the working groups.

WS-I Deliverables

The WS-I provides four types of deliverables. These are:

- Profiles
- Test tools
- Use cases and usage scenarios
- Sample applications

Profiles

Profiles were created by the WS-I in response to the ever-growing number of interrelated specifications, all at different version levels and differing stages of development and adoption, and often with conflicting requirements. The group determined that developers needed some way of knowing which products supported what levels of specification. Profiles solve this problem. They contain lists of named and versioned Web services specifications, along with implementation and interoperability guidelines that recommend how the specified components should be used together to develop interoperable Web services.

Presently, there is one profile available called the Basic Profile. The Basic Profile deals with the following components:

- Messaging (SOAP/HTTP), which is the exchange of protocol elements, usually over a network, to allow Web service interfaces to communicate with each other.
- Description (WSDL), which is the mechanism through which Web service definitions are exposed and to which Web service implementers must conform when sending SOAP messages.
- Discovery (UDDI), which is the metadata enabling the advertisement of a Web service.
- XML Schema, which is how data definitions are structured in a SOAP document.
- XML 1.0, which is how XML data is serialized to a network stream or a file.

Test Tools

The test tools consist of a monitor and an analyzer. The monitor intercepts and records interactions either between Web services or with a Web service, treating the Web service and components with which it communicates as black boxes. It generates a log that is later processed by the analyzer. The analyzer verifies that the intercepted Web service interactions recorded in the log conform to a given profile. As input, it uses the implementation guideline assertions from the profile, WSDL and/or UDDI descriptions of the Web service under test, and the logs generated by the monitor. The analyzer's focus is on detecting instances where a Web service deviates from the profile rather than on verifying that every feature of a particular profile was implemented in the Web service.

Use Cases and Usage Scenarios

Within the context of a particular profile, use cases and usage scenarios capture, respectively, the business and technical requirements for using Web services in a particular situation. For the Basic Profile, these requirements were used by the sample applications group to produce a *Technical Design and Implementation Specification* for a sample application that describes the Web services needed, along with the necessary supporting resources such as WSDL files, XML schema, and UDDI Web service registrations. Use cases are provided that provide a framework for demonstrating the guidelines described in the profiles.

Sample Applications

Sample applications are implementations of applications that are built from use cases and usage scenarios. These implementations are expected for each of the major platforms currently available. Once development is nearly complete, members of the implementation working group will cross-test them to see if they are interoperable. Any problems that arise will be communicated to the profile group so that they can revise their documentation.

More Information

The Microsoft Developer's Network (MSDN) has a site specifically for Web services developers called the XML Web Services Developer Center at *http://www.msdn.microsoft.com/webservices/default.aspx*. Some articles of immediate interest are:

- The Web Services Idea at *http://www.msdn.microsoft.com/webservices/understanding/readme/default.aspx*
- Understanding Namespaces at *http://www.msdn.microsoft.com/webservices/default.aspx?pull=/library/en-us/dnxml/html/xml_namespaces.asp*
- Getting Started with XML Web Services in Visual Studio .NET at *http://www.msdn.microsoft.com/webservices/default.aspx?pull=/library/en-us/dv_vstechart/html/vbtchGettingStartedWithXMLWebServicesInVisualStudioNET.asp*
- RPC/Literal and Freedom of Choice at *http://msdn.microsoft.com/library/default.asp?url=/library/en-us/dnwebsrv/html/rpc_literal.asp*
- The Argument Against SOAP Encoding at *http://msdn.microsoft.com/library/default.asp?url=/library/en-us/dnsoap/html/argsoape.asp*

2

The WS-I Deliverables

Introduction

This chapter describes the four deliverables produced by the WS-I for the Basic Profile version 1.0. Briefly, they are:

- The Basic Profile, which contains requirements and guidelines for writing interoperable Web services.
- The Basic Profile usage scenarios, which describe fundamental ways that providers and consumers interact.
- The sample application, which is an implementation of an interoperable Web service that demonstrates the requirements and guidelines presented in the Basic Profile.
- The testing tools, which help developers verify that their Web service implementations conform to the requirements in the Basic Profile.

We shall discuss each of these deliverables in more detail in the following sections. The WS-I Basic Profile, sample application, and test tools are available at *http://www.ws-i.org*.

The Basic Profile

The Basic Profile consists of a set of constraints and guidelines that, if followed, will help developers write interoperable Web services. Together, these guidelines and constraints represent the WS-I's approach toward interoperability. This approach is based on some underlying principles, which we will discuss in this section.

Scope of the Profile

The *scope* of the profile is defined by a group of specifications at particular version levels. Currently, the profile's scope includes the following specifications:

- Simple Object Access Protocol (SOAP) 1.1 (*http://www.w3.org/TR/SOAP/*)
- Extensible Markup Language (XML) 1.0 (Second Edition) (*http://www.w3.org/TR/REC-xml*)
- RFC2616: Hypertext Transfer Protocol—HTTP/1.1 (*http://www.ietf.org/rfc/rfc2616*)
- RFC2965: HTTP State Management Mechanism (*http://www.ietf.org/rfc/rfc2965*)
- Web Services Description Language (WSDL) 1.1 (*http://www.w3.org/TR/wsdl.html*)
- XML Schema Part 1: Structures (*http://www.w3.org/TR/xmlschema-1*)
- XML Schema Part 2: Datatypes (*http://www.w3.org/TR/xmlschema-2*)
- UDDI Version 2.04 API Specification, Dated 19 July 2002 (*http://uddi.org/pubs/ProgrammersAPI-V2.04-Published-20020719.htm*)
- UDDI Version 2.03 Data Structure Reference, Dated 19 July 2002 (*http://uddi.org/pubs/DataStructure-V2.03-Published-20020719.htm*)
- UDDI Version 2 XML Schema (*http://uddi.org/schema/uddi_v2.xsd*)
- RFC2818: HTTP Over TLS (*http://www.ietf.org/rfc/rfc2818*)
- RFC2246: The TLS Protocol Version 1.0 (*http://www.ietf.org/rfc/rfc2246*)
- The SSL Protocol Version 3.0 (*http://wp.netscape.com/eng/ssl3/draft302.txt*)
- RFC2459: Internet X.509 Public Key Infrastructure Certificate and CRL Profile (*http://www.ietf.org/rfc/rfc2459*)

Specifications often provide ways of extending the components they describe to increase their capabilities. For example, the SOAP 1.1 specification states that typical examples of extensions that can be implemented as header entries are authentication, transaction management, and payment methods. These extensions allow vendors to introduce products that are both uniquely their own and that still interoperate with other Web services. To promote this flexibility, the Basic Profile never imposes limitations on the range of these extensions. For a complete list of the profile's extensibility points, see Appendix II of the Basic Profile.

Level of Granularity

The profile addresses interoperability at the application layer and relies on well-understood lower-layer protocols such as TCP/IP, and Ethernet. It assumes that protocols such as SSL/TLS and HTTP are also well understood and only mentions them specifically when there is an issue that affects Web services. It is important to note that WS-I does not address all issues, but only those that are related to interoperability of Web services.

Profile Conformance

Conformance to the profile means adherence to specifications that comprise the profile's scope and to the profile's *requirements*. Requirements are the rules that any Web service must adhere to in order to meet the profile's standards for interoperability. Each requirement is individually identified by the letter "R" and a number, such as R1000.

There are two types of conformance. The most basic type is conformance at the level of an *artifact*. Artifacts are the primary elements of any Web service. The profile has rules about three types of artifacts:

- Messages, which are protocol elements that are exchanged (usually over a network) to effect a Web service (for example, SOAP/HTTP messages). The scope of conformance is the entire message.
- Descriptions, which are descriptions of types, messages, interfaces and their concrete protocol and data format bindings, and the network access points associated with Web services (for example, WSDL descriptions). The scope of conformance is **wsdl:port**, or parts of a port.
- REGDATA, which are statements about Web services that are used to discover their capabilities (for example, UDDI tModels). The scope of conformance is **bindingTemplate** or **tModels**.

An artifact is conformant when all of the profile's requirements associated with that artifact type are met.

A second, higher-level of conformance, is called conformance of services and consumers. This occurs when a Web service both produces and consumes only conformant artifacts. If multiple types of a particular artifact are possible, a conformant service must be able to consume them all. For example, while a sender may encode XML in UTF-8 or UTF-16 when sending a message, a receiver must be capable of using either one.

Where possible, the profile places requirements on artifacts (for example, WSDL descriptions and SOAP messages) rather than on the producing or consuming software's behaviors or roles. Artifacts are concrete, making them easier to verify and therefore making conformance easier to understand and less error-prone.

Strength of Requirements

The profile makes strong requirements (for example, MUST, and MUST NOT) wherever possible. If there are times when a strong requirement cannot be met, conditional requirements (for example, SHOULD, and SHOULD NOT) are used. If the requirements are going to be amended, they may become more restrictive but they will not become looser. For example, the profile will not change a MUST to a MAY.

Testability

When possible, the profile makes statements that are testable but testability is not a requirement for a statement. The profile suggests that, preferably, testing should be performed in non-intrusive ways such as examining artifacts "on the wire." An example of this is the monitor, which is a test tool provided by the WS-I. It is described later in this chapter.

Multiple Mechanisms

If one of the profile's specifications allows a variety of mechanisms to be used interchangeably, the profile uses the ones that are best understood and most widely implemented. This is because underspecified or little-known mechanisms and extensions can introduce complexity and, therefore, may reduce interoperability.

Compatibility

Although backward compatibility isn't an explicit goal of the Basic Profile, it tries to avoid introducing changes to the requirements of a specification unless doing so addresses specific interoperability issues. Also, where possible, the profile's requirements are compatible with in-progress revisions to the specifications it references (for example, SOAP 1.2 or WSDL 1.2).

Application Semantics

Application semantics basically lie outside of the profile. By application semantics we mean definitions of what an application does. For example, an airlines reservations Web service will have the format of a message request defined, but whether that message charges a credit card or sends tickets through the mail isn't specified.

Basic Profile Usage Scenarios

The Basic Profile usage scenarios define how Web services are used in specific types of interactions between a consumer and a provider. They identify the basic interoperability requirements for these interactions and map them to the requirements of the Basic Profile.

The scenarios reflect fundamental, real-world Web service requirements. They can be combined and built upon like building blocks. For example, the Synchronous Request/Response scenario describes a basic exchange that can be expanded by adding SOAP headers. The only requirement is that the extensions must also conform to the Basic Profile.

The WS-I has defined three usage scenarios to complement the Basic Profile:

- One-way usage scenario
- Synchronous request/response usage scenario
- Basic callback usage scenario

One-way Usage Scenario

In the one-way usage scenario, a consumer sends a message to a provider. The provider receives the message and processes it but doesn't generate a response in return. The following diagram illustrates this case:

Figure 2.1
One-way usage scenario

At the highest level, the flow can be broken down into 2 steps:

1. The consumer invokes the service by sending a SOAP message bound to an HTTP request to the provider.
2. The provider executes the service.

Synchronous Request/Response Scenario

In the synchronous request/response usage scenario, the consumer first sends a message to the provider. The provider processes it and simultaneously sends back a response. The following diagram illustrates this case:

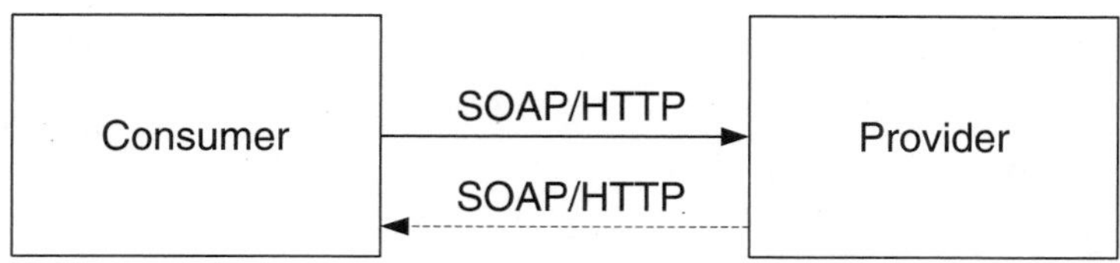

Figure 2.2
Synchronous request/response scenario

At the highest level, the flow can be broken down into 2 steps:

1. The consumer invokes the service by sending a SOAP message bound to an HTTP request to the provider.
2. The provider executes the service and sends a SOAP message bound to an HTTP response to the consumer.

Basic Callback

The basic callback usage scenario employs a type of asynchronous message exchange for Web services using two synchronous request/response pairs (see the previous section for more information). Since both the consumer and the provider may have other outstanding requests, the consumer adds some type of data, such as a purchase order number, that the provider can use to associate the correct response with the correct request. An alternative approach is to use some form of message ID. In addition, the consumer also supplies the provider with the endpoint information for the callback service. This service is defined by the provider in the published Web service description and is implemented by the consumer. The following diagram illustrates this case:

Figure 2.3
Basic callback

At the highest level, the flow can be broken down into 4 steps:

1. The consumer initiates the service by sending a SOAP message bound to an HTTP request to the provider. This is the initial request.
2. The provider acknowledges receipt by sending a SOAP message bound to an HTTP response to the consumer. This is the initial response.
3. The provider completes the exchange by sending a SOAP message bound to an HTTP request to the consumer with the results of the initial request. This is the final request, or callback.
4. The consumer acknowledges receipt of the callback message with a SOAP message bound to an HTTP response. This is the final response.

Note: For more information on these usage scenarios, including detailed flows, see the WS-I Usage Scenarios paper available at *http://www.ws-i.org/*.

The WS-I Basic Profile Sample Application

In addition to the Basic Profile, the WS-I has also created a Basic Profile sample application. The sample application demonstrates all of the scenarios in the Basic Profile as well as providing an example of how the Basic Profile allows Web services from different vendors to interoperate.

The WS-I Basic Profile sample application is a supply-chain management application that models a retailer selling electronics. The retailer has three warehouses and sells goods from three manufacturers. When using the sample application, a user can select different vendor implementations for each of the warehouses and manufacturers to observe how the Basic Profile allows Web services to interoperate. In addition, there is a logging facility so that the activity generated by the Web services can be logged.

For more information on the WS-I Basic Profile sample application, see the WS-I Supply Chain Management Use Cases and Supply Chain Management Sample Architecture papers available at *http://www.ws-i.org* as well as the Microsoft sample application available at *http://ws-i.gotdotnet.com/wsi/webclient/*.

The WS-I Basic Profile Test Tools

The WS-I has developed two test tools, a monitor and an analyzer, that are used in conjunction with each other for evaluating whether or not a Web service follows the Basic Profile guidelines. Both C# and Java versions of the tools are available. Briefly, the tools do the following:

- The monitor captures and logs the messages between a Web service and a consumer.
- The analyzer examines the messages logged by the monitor and analyzes them as to whether or not a Web service follows the Basic Profile guidelines.

The following diagram shows the relationship between the monitor and the analyzer:

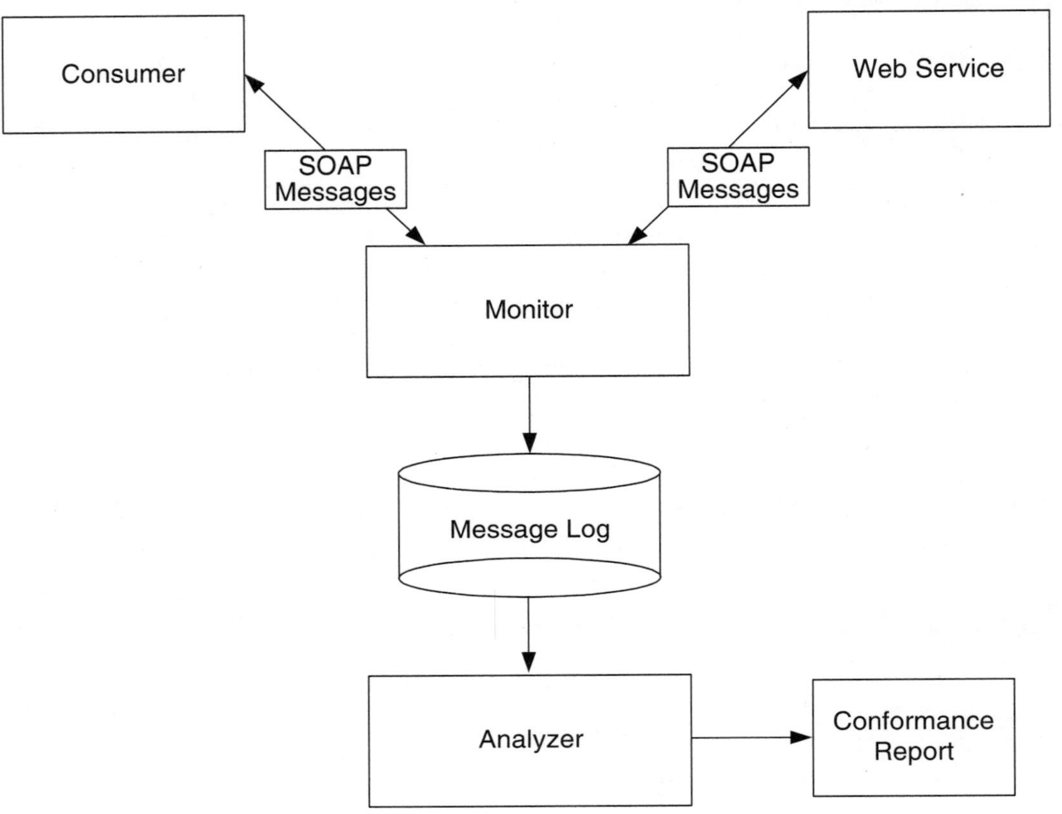

Figure 2.4
The WSI test tools

The Monitor

The monitor uses a *man in the middle* approach, meaning it sits between the consumer and the Web service, intercepting all the SOAP/HTTP messages they exchange. The messages are stored in a log file for later use by the analyzer. The following diagram describes them monitor:

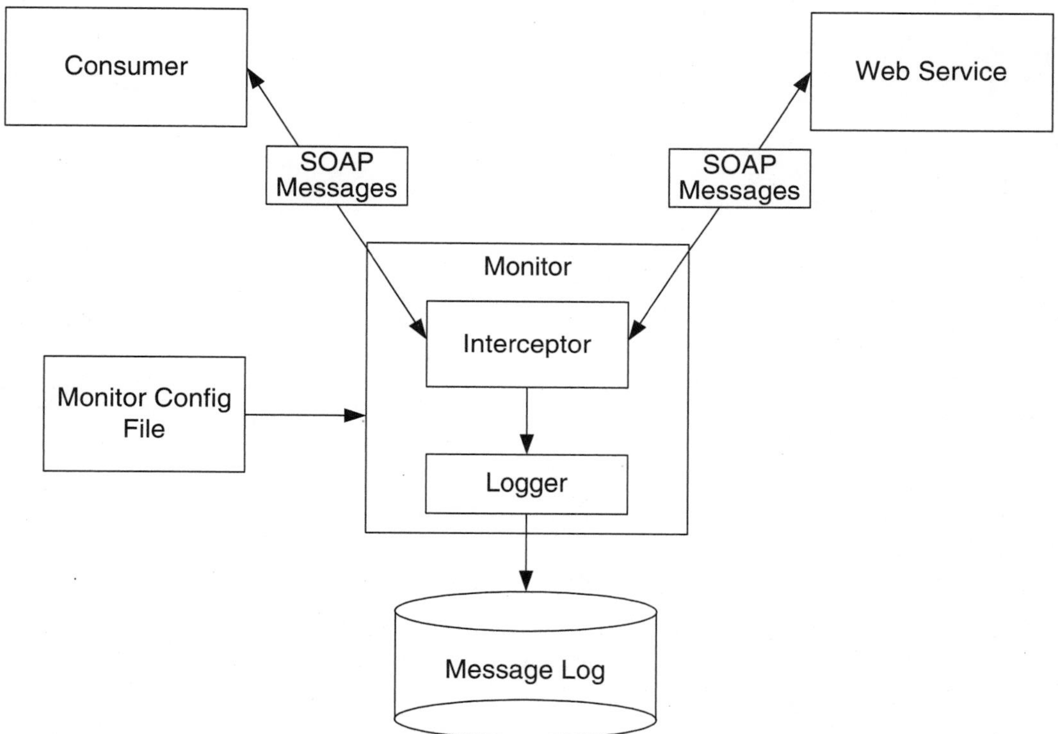

Figure 2.5
The monitor

The monitor configuration file is an XML document that controls the operation of the monitor and defines the parameters that ensure that the SOAP messages are properly routed.

Note: For more information on the contents of the monitor configuration file, see the Test Tools User guide available at *http://www.ws-i.org/*.

The Analyzer

The analyzer uses the monitor's log files as input and analyzes the following items:

- Descriptions, which are WSDL data.
- Messages, which are HTTP message items from the XML message log file.
- Discovery data, which is comprised of the UDDI entries.

The following diagram illustrates how the analyzer works:

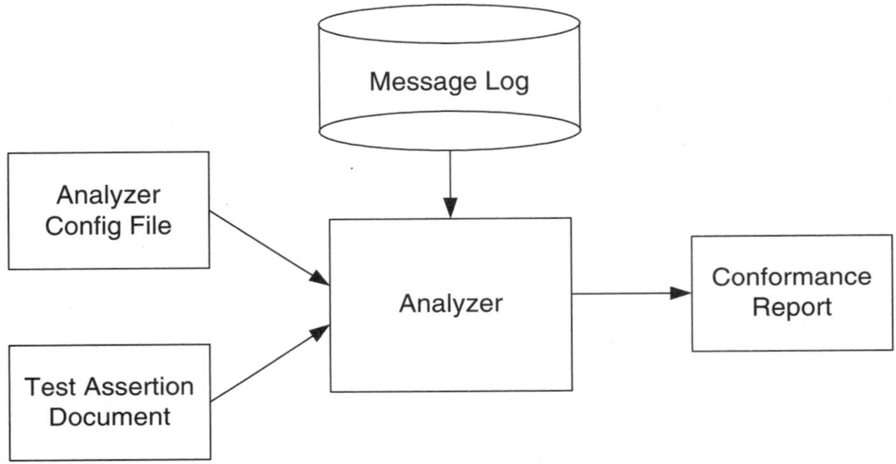

Figure 2.6
The analyzer

Similarly to the monitor, the analyzer also has a configuration file that contains the list of options for the tool as well as possibly containing implementation-specific configuration parameters.

The analyzer also uses the test assertion document. This document encodes the Basic Profile's rules. The analyzer compares the Web service under test to the requirements in the test assertion document to see if the Web service complies with the Basic Profile's rules.

Note: For more information on the analyzer files, see the Test Tools User guide available at *http://www.ws-i.org/*.

Once it has completed analyzing the log files, the analyzer issues a conformance report. The overall result of the report will be that the implementation either passed or failed. It is important to remember that, because the test tools only examine the messages between a web service and a requestor, they do not test all requirements of the Basic Profile. This is why the tools are said to evaluate conformance and not certify a Web service. For more information on the WS-I Basic Profile test tools, see the user's guide available at *http://www.ws-i.org*.

More Information

The WS-I Basic Profile, sample application, and test tools at *http://www.ws-i.org/Documents.aspx*.

3

How to Apply the Basic Profile

This chapter details some best practice recommendations. These recommendations explain how to use Visual Studio.NET to create Web services and Web service clients that conform to the Basic Profile. Some recommendations are general guidelines while others apply to particular directives in the Basic Profile. If a recommendation does apply to particular directives, their numbers are listed in square brackets after the recommendation (for example, [R1120]). There are two other types of recommendations:

- Recommendations that apply when using Visual Studio.NET to create a Web service
- Recommendations that apply when using Visual Studio.NET to create a Web service client that consumes Web services

Recommendations for Creating Web Services

The most common way of creating a Web service with Visual Studio.NET, and also the easiest starting point for creating a Web service that complies with the Basic Profile, is by implementing it as an ASMX page. This is what automatically is created when you use the **Add New Project** wizard to generate a new ASP.NET Web service project. The following recommendations assume this method of creating a Web service.

You must consider the following when creating a Web service that complies with the Basic Profile:

- Parameter types
- Extensibility mechanisms
- Conformance claims
- Cookies
- Encoding

- Redirection
- The **WebServiceBinding** attribute
- The **SoapDocumentMethod** attribute and the **SoapDocumentService** attribute
- SOAP headers
- Exception handling

Parameter Types

If your Web service includes parameters, headers, or return types that allow complex types, then you must ensure that the XML schema generation or serialization based on your usage of the complex type does not violate any of the Basic Profile rules. An example would be a return type of **XmlNode**, which would allow any possible XML to be returned, so does not restrict you from including **soap:encodingStyle** attributes.

Extensibility Mechanisms

The .NET framework offers multiple extensibility mechanisms that can modify Web service behavior such as **SoapExtension**, **IHttpModule**, **IHttpHandler**, and **SoapExtensionReflector**. These types of extensibility mechanisms give you low-level control over the SOAP or HTTP response, or the WSDL generation. When using these types of extensibility mechanisms, you'll need to review the Basic Profile rules directly to check if, for example, a modification to the SOAP response is in conflict with a Basic Profile rule. The WS-I Basic Profile test tools can also be used to help ensure compliance when using an extensibility mechanism.

Conformance Claims

The Basic Profile describes how to include conformance claims in your WSDL description although it is optional to include them. A .NET Web service does not support including a conformance claim when it generates a WSDL description. To include a conformance claim in the WSDL for your Web service, the easiest method is to save the auto-generated WSDL and then manually modify it to add any conformance claims. [R0002][R0003]

Cookies

The Basic Profile does not prohibit using cookies but says that, if you do use them, they should only be used for optimization purposes and should not be required for the Web service to function correctly. [R1120][R1121]

Microsoft recommends that you do not use cookies in your Web service. Any data sent between the client and your Web service should be in the SOAP request or response message itself. Also, Web service implementations would not be able to forward the SOAP message to another processor using a protocol other then HTTP because cookies are only supported by the HTTP protocol.

Encoding

Do not use either the **SoapRpcService** or **SoapRpcMethod** attributes in your Web service because the Basic Profile does not allow **RPC/Encoded**. Similarly, when you use the **SoapDocumentMethod** or the **SoapDocumentService** attributes do not set the **Use** property to **SoapBindingUse.Encoded** because the Basic Profile does not allow **Document/Encoded**. [R1005][R1006][R2706]

RPC/Literal

A .NET Web service does not support generating a WSDL description with an RPC/Literal binding. Also, .NET does not provide explicit support for creating a Web service that accepts messages described by an RPC/Literal binding although you can still create a .NET Web service that will accept such a message. [R1007][R2203][R2211][R2705][R2706][R2717][R2726][R2729][R2735][R2737]

Microsoft recommends using Document/Literal in describing and implementing your Web service. Microsoft tools provide much better support for Document/Literal then RPC/Literal. Generally, the intended difference between RPC/Literal and Document/Literal binding is the programming model that each implies (RPC vs. messaging). However, there is no difference in terms of the real data that can be sent or the actual programming model that can be used. Document/Literal does offer the benefit of allowing the entire SOAP body to be validated using a single XSD schema.

Note: For more information on RPC/Literal, see the More Information section at the end of this chapter.

Here is a sample WSDL description with an RPC/Literal binding, and a .NET Web service that can accept messages described by the WSDL:

```
WSDL:
<?xml version="1.0" encoding="utf-8"?>
<definitions
    xmlns:soap="http://schemas.xmlsoap.org/wsdl/soap/"
    xmlns:s="http://www.w3.org/2001/XMLSchema"
    xmlns:s0="http://msdn.microsoft.com/practices"
    targetNamespace="http://msdn.microsoft.com/practices"
    xmlns="http://schemas.xmlsoap.org/wsdl/">

  <types>
    <s:schema elementFormDefault="qualified"
targetNamespace="http://msdn.microsoft.com/practices">
      <s:complexType name="Param1Type">
        <s:sequence>
          <s:element minOccurs="0" maxOccurs="1"
name="FirstValue" type="s:string" />
          <s:element minOccurs="0" maxOccurs="1"
```

(continued)

(continued)

```
name="SecondValue" type="s:string" />
        </s:sequence>
      </s:complexType>
      <s:complexType name="Param2Type">
        <s:sequence>
          <s:element minOccurs="0" maxOccurs="1"
name="FirstValue" type="s:string" />
          <s:element minOccurs="0" maxOccurs="1"
name="SecondValue" type="s:string" />
        </s:sequence>
      </s:complexType>
    </s:schema>
  </types>

  <message name="HelloWorldSoapIn">
    <part name="param1" type="s0:Param1Type" />
    <part name="param2" type="s0:Param2Type" />
  </message>
  <message name="HelloWorldSoapOut">
    <part name="HelloWorldResult" type="s:string" />
  </message>

  <portType name="MyWebServiceSoap">
    <operation name="HelloWorld">
      <input message="s0:HelloWorldSoapIn" />
      <output message="s0:HelloWorldSoapOut" />
    </operation>
  </portType>

  <binding name="MyWebServiceSoap" type="s0:MyWebServiceSoap">
    <soap:binding transport="http://schemas.xmlsoap.org/soap/http"
style="rpc" />
    <operation name="HelloWorld">
      <soap:operation style="rpc" />
      <input>
        <soap:body use="literal"
namespace="http://msdn.microsoft.com/practices" />
      </input>
      <output>
        <soap:body use="literal"
namespace="http://msdn.microsoft.com/practices" />
      </output>
    </operation>
  </binding>

  <service name="MyWebService">
    <port name="MyWebServiceSoap" binding="s0:MyWebServiceSoap">
      <soap:address
location="http://localhost/WebServices/MyWebService.asmx" />
    </port>
  </service>
</definitions>
```

(continued)

(continued)

```
.NET Web service:
[WebService(Namespace="http://msdn.microsoft.com/practices")]
public class Service1 : System.Web.Services.WebService
{

    [WebMethod]
    [SoapDocumentMethod(ParameterStyle=SoapParameterStyle.Bare)]
    [return: XmlElement(Namespace="")]
    public string HelloWorld(HelloWorldRequestType HelloWorld)
    {
        return "Hello World";
    }
}

[XmlType(Namespace="")]
public class HelloWorldRequestType
{
    public Param1Type param1;
    public Param2Type param2;
}

[XmlType(Namespace="http://msdn.microsoft.com/practices")]
public class Param1Type
{
    public string FirstValue;
    public string SecondValue;
}

[XmlType(Namespace="http://msdn.microsoft.com/practices")]
public class Param2Type
{
    public string FirstValue;
    public string SecondValue;
}
```

Redirection

If you need to provide a redirect response in your Web service, do not use the **Context.Response.Redirect** method because the HTTP response will differ from what the Basic Profile mandates. [R1130]

The following example shows how to give a redirect response that complies with the Basic Profile:

```
[WebMethod]
public string HelloWorld()
{
  Context.Response.StatusCode = 307;
  Context.Response.AddHeader("Location","<redirect URL>");
  return null;
}
```

WebServiceBindingAttribute

When using a **WebServiceBindingAttribute** for importing a WSDL description, there are two restrictions you must follow to ensure that the WSDL generated by your .NET Web service does not violate any Basic Profile rules.

First, you must specify the **Location** property with a non-empty value. Otherwise, the WSDL generated will include a WSDL import statement which imports an XSD schema. [R2007]

Second, the **Namespace** property value must match the value of the **targetNamespace** attribute on the **wsdl:definitions** element in the WSDL description that is specified by the **Location** property of the **WebServiceBindingAttribute**. [R2005]

SoapDocumentMethodAttribute & SoapDocumentServiceAttribute

When using a **SoapDocumentMethodAttribute** or **SoapDocumentServiceAttribute** there are certain restrictions if you set the **ParameterStyle** property to **SoapParameterStyle.Bare**. These restrictions are you must not have more then one parameter to your **WebMethod**, and no two **WebMethods** can have identical parameters. [R2210][R2710]

SOAP Headers

When using a **SoapHeaderAttribute**, do not set the **Direction** property to **SoapHeaderDirection.Fault** or the WSDL description generated by your .NET Web service will include a **soapbind:header** element for the **wsdl:output**, which will not be included in the response messages from your Web service. [R2738]

The Basic Profile requires that any headers received by a Web service that are marked as mandatory must be validated before any processing can occur. Even if there are no headers declared for the Web service itself, the caller of the Web service might send headers that are marked as mandatory. These headers must also be checked. You can check for undeclared headers that have been sent by a caller by adding a **SoapHeaderAttribute** to a variable typed as an array of **SoapUnknownHeader**. [R1025][R1027][R2739][R2753][R2725]

This example shows how to check both a defined header called "myHeader" and any undefined headers the caller may have sent by using an "unknownHeaders" header:

```
public MyHeaderType myHeader;
public SoapUnknownHeader[] unknownHeaders;

[WebMethod]
[SoapHeader("myHeader", Required=false)]
[SoapHeader("unknownHeaders", Required=false)]
public string HelloWorld()
```

(continued)

(continued)

```
{
    bool isHeadersValid = true;

    // Check if declared header is marked as mandatory
    if (myHeader.MustUnderstand == true)
    {
        // Validate the information in the declared header
        if (<validation test of myHeader data> == false)
        {
            myHeader.DidUnderstand = false;
            isHeadersValid = false;
        }
    }

    // Check for unknown headers marked as mandatory
    foreach (SoapUnknownHeader header in unknownHeaders)
    {
        if (header.MustUnderstand)
        {
            header.DidUnderstand = false;
            isHeadersValid = false;
        }
    }
    if (isHeadersValid == false)
    {
        // exit method before processing
        return null;
    }
    // Execute normal web service processing
}
```

Exception Handling

Any exception thrown in a .NET Web service that is not of type **SoapException** is automatically wrapped in a **SoapException** by the .NET framework. In turn, the **SoapException** will then be converted to a SOAP fault message that is returned to the caller of the Web service. Because the Basic Profile has restrictions on SOAP fault messages, there are restrictions on how you throw a **SoapException** so that, when the .NET framework generates the SOAP Fault message, it does not violate any rules of the Basic Profile. These restrictions concern both the **Code** property and the **Detail** property.

The Code Property

The Basic Profile does not require, but does recommend that you use a namespace qualified fault code or one of the four fields of the **SoapException** class to set the code property. Specifically, these fields are the **SoapException.VersionMismatchFaultCode**, the **SoapException.MustUnderstandFaultCode**, the **SoapException.ClientFaultCode**, and the **SoapException.ServerFaultCode**. [R1004]

The Detail Property

When the detail property is specified, the root node element must be created using the **SoapException.DetailElementName** values. [R1000][R1001]

Here is an example:

```
XmlDocument doc = new Document();
// detail node is required to be the parent element
XmlNode detail = doc.CreateNode(XmlNodeType.Element,
SoapException.DetailElementName.Name, SoapException.DetailElementName.Namespace);
// Add additional child nodes here
throw new SoapException("MyFault", SoapException.ServerFaultCode, "MyActor",
detail);
```

You are not allowed to add attributes to the detail node with the namespace "http://schemas.xmlsoap.org/soap/envelope/". [R1003]

Here is an example of what not to do:

```
detail.Attributes.Append(doc.CreateAttribute("soap", "MyAttribute",
"http://schemas.xmlsoap.org/soap/envelope/"));
```

Recommendations for Creating Web Service Clients

The most common way of creating a Web service client with Visual Studio.NET is to use the **Add Web Reference** wizard, which reads the WSDL description of the Web service and auto-generates a proxy class that inherits from the **SoapHttpClientProcotol** class. The following information assumes this is how you create your Web service client, and also assumes the Web service and its WSDL are Basic Profile compliant. Issues you must consider when creating a Web service client that complies with the Basic Profile fall into two categories. One category is what happens when you invoke a Web service using an auto-generated proxy class. The other is using the **Add Web Reference** wizard. We will discuss each in turn.

Invoking the Web Service Using the Proxy Class

When you invoke a Web service, you must consider the following issues:

- Conformance claims
- Message format
- Parameter types
- Cookies
- One-way operations
- SOAP headers

Conformance Claims

The Basic Profile describes how to include conformance claims in your message although it is optional to include them. A proxy class generated by the Add Web Reference wizard will not include WS-I conformance claims in messages sent to the Web service. [R0004][R0005][R0006][R0007]

To include conformance claims you will need to manually modify the proxy class to make it support including a conformance claim header. You must also make sure to set the header property (ClaimHeaderValue in this example) to a valid instance of the header and not set the MustUnderstand property before invoking the Web service. The following shows the code necessary to add to the proxy class to make it support including a conformance claim:

```
// Add the following to the variable declarations
// of the proxy
public ClaimHeaderType ClaimHeaderValue;

// Add the following immediately before the WebMethod
[SoapHeaderAttribute("ClaimHeaderValue")]

// Add the following class at the end of the file
 [XmlRoot ("Claim",
Namespace="http://ws-i.org/schemas/conformanceClaim/",
IsNullable=false)]
public class ClaimHeaderType : SoapHeader
{
  [XmlAttribute ()]
  public string conformsTo = "http://ws-i.org/profiles/basic/1.0";
}
```

Message Format

When calling a Web service, the default message serialization format is UTF-8. The **SoapHttpClientProtocol** class allows you to override this by setting the **RequestEncoding** property. Since the Basic Profile permits either UTF-8 or UTF-16 encoding, you can set this property to either **UTF8Encoding** or **UnicodeEncoding** (which is the same as UTF-16). [R1012]

Parameter Types

If a parameter or SOAP header value of the Web service allows complex types, then you must ensure that your usage of the complex type does not result in a serialized form when passing, which would violate any of the Basic Profile rules. An example would be a parameter type of **XmlNode**, which would allow any possible XML to be passed, so would not restrict you from including **soap:encodingStyle** attributes.

Cookies

If, when calling a Web service, any cookies are returned in the **CookieContainer** property, you must not use the values of the cookies for any purpose other then passing them back to the Web service in additional calls. [R1123]

One-Way Operations

The Basic Profile requires the consumer to ignore the SOAP response for a one-way operation; however in an error condition the proxy class will read the response to include in the details of the **SoapException**. Your client code must ignore the details in any **SoapException** when invoking a one-way operation. [R2750]

If, when calling a Web service, the method is a one-way operation, you must also not write your application so that it interprets a successful response to mean that the message was valid or that the receiver will process it. [R2727]

SOAP Headers

When invoking a method of the proxy class, all **SoapHeader** properties of the proxy class that are used by that method must first be initialized with an instance of the header. [R2738]

Using the Add Web Reference wizard

The following cover issues related to the **Add Web Reference** wizard's reading of a WSDL description.

Conformance Claims

The **Add Web Reference** wizard fails if a WSDL description contains WS-I conformance claims. You'll need to manually edit the WSDL to remove the conformance claims before using the **Add Web Reference** wizard. [R0002][R0003]

Required WSDL Extension Elements

The Basic Profile requires that all WSDL extension elements marked as **required** must not be ignored when processing the WSDL. However, the **Add Web Reference** wizard ignores any WSDL extension elements it does not recognize, even if they are marked as **required**. You must review the WSDL first to see if any such elements exist. You can also use the wsdl.exe command line tool which displays warnings if it finds WSDL elements marked as **required**. [R2027]

WSDL Description Encoding

The Basic Profile allows WSDL descriptions to be encoded in either UTF-8 or UTF-16. However, the **Add Web Reference** wizard in Visual Studio.NET only supports UTF-8 encoded WSDL descriptions. If the WSDL description is encoded with UTF-16, you must manually convert it to UTF-8 before using the **Add Web Reference** wizard. Notepad.exe can be used for converting because it supports opening a UTF-16 document, and using the **Save As** dialog, saving in ANSI format. [R4003]

RPC-Literal Binding in WSDL Description

The Basic Profile allows WSDL descriptions to have RPC-Literal bindings. However, the **Add Web Reference** wizard in Visual Studio.NET does not support WSDL descriptions with RPC-Literal bindings. You can manually create a class which inherits from **SoapHttpClientProtocol** and uses the **SoapDocumentMethodAttribute** with a **ParameterStyle** of **SoapParameterStyle.Bare** on your **WebMethod**s. Alternatively, you can edit the WSDL description to convert it to a Document-Literal binding (see "RPC/Literal and Freedom of Choice" under More Information). [R1007][R2203][R2208][R2211][R2705][R2717][R2726][R2729][R2735][R2737]

The following example shows how to create such a class. Using the same WSDL description example that is in the RPC/Literal section of this chapter, this example is the C# code (including the class which inherits from the **SoapHttpClientProtocol** class), which allows you to use the WSDL description with an RPC-Literal binding.

```
SoapHttpClientProtocol inherited class -
[WebServiceBinding(Name="MyWebServiceSoap",
Namespace="http://msdn.microsoft.com/practices")]
public class MyWebService : SoapHttpClientProtocol {

    public MyWebService() {
        this.Url = "http://localhost/WebServices/MyWebService.asmx";
    }

    [SoapDocumentMethod("http://msdn.microsoft.com/practices/HelloWorld",
ParameterStyle=SoapParameterStyle.Bare)]
    [return: XmlElement(Namespace="")]
    public string HelloWorld([XmlElement("HelloWorld",
Namespace="http://msdn.microsoft.com/practices")] HelloWorldRequestType
HelloWorld1) {
        object[] results = this.Invoke("HelloWorld", new object[] {
                        HelloWorld1});
        return ((string)(results[0]));
    }
}
```

(continued)

(continued)

```
[XmlType(Namespace="http://msdn.microsoft.com/practices")]
public class Param2Type {
    public string FirstValue;
    public string SecondValue;
}

[XmlType(Namespace="http://msdn.microsoft.com/practices")]
public class Param1Type {
    public string FirstValue;
    public string SecondValue;
}

[XmlType(Namespace="")]
public class HelloWorldRequestType {
    public Param1Type param1;
    public Param2Type param2;
}
```

More Information

The WS-I Basic Profile 1.0 (*http://www.ws-i.org/Documents.asp*)

RPC/Literal and Freedom of Choice (*http://msdn.microsoft.com/library/default.asp?url=/nhp/default.asp?contentid=28000438*)

4

Applying Basic Profile Rules When Implementing Web Services

Developers who write Web services may find that they need to adjust their code to make it comply with the constraints included in the Basic Profile. To provide some guidance on how to make these adjustments, we first made some general assumptions about how a developer will implement a Web service.

These assumptions are made for the purposes of this chapter because otherwise they would apply very broadly. For example, if the usage of **SoapExtensions** were considered for each rule, then a large portion of the rules would be listed as potentially compliant since a custom **SoapExtension** allows very flexible control of Web service behavior allowing for violation of the rule.

These assumptions are:

- The Web service is implemented as a class derived from the .NET **WebService** class. When you use the Visual Studio .NET **Add New Project** wizard, it generates a template class derived from the **WebService** class when it creates an ASP.NET Web service project.
- Parameters, return values, and headers do not contain **XmlNode** types or complex data types that when serialized violate a rule.
- The Web service doesn't use any custom **SoapExtension** or **IHttpHandler** classes, or custom **HttpModule** assemblies to modify the HTTP or SOAP response.
- The Web service doesn't use any custom **SoapExtensionReflector** classes to modify the way the WSDL is generated.

Next, we assigned each of the Basic Profile rules one of four possible levels of compliance. These levels indicate how closely a Web service written according to our assumptions complies with the rules' requirements. The levels are:

- Compliant—this means that if the particular profile rule is applicable to your Web service, you do not need to make any code changes to meet the rule's requirements. Note that "weak" rules that contain SHOULD or MAY are classified as compliant when the Web service does not meet their requirements. This is because these rules aren't mandatory. For an example, see R2740.
- Typically compliant—this means that if the particular profile rule is applicable to your Web service, it probably meets the requirements of the rule but there is a possibility it needs code adjustments.
- Potentially compliant—this means that if the particular profile rule is applicable to your Web service, you will probably need to make code adjustments to make your Web service meet the rule's requirements.
- Unique—this means that if the profile rule is applicable to your Web service, you will need to make code adjustments by using **SoapExtension**, **HttpModule**, or other unusual means to meet the rule's requirements.

All the rules are included in the same groups (such as messaging) and order as they are listed in the Basic Profile. Note that only the rule numbers and directives are included. For the complete text, consult the WS-I Basic Profile at *http://www.ws-i.org/Profiles/Basic/2002-10/BasicProfile-1.0-WGD.htm*. The next entry after the rule is the level of compliancy and the final entry includes comments, suggestions and code samples. Here is an example of the format:

R0001 ← Profile rule number

An INSTANCE MUST be described by a WSDL 1.1 service description, by a UDDI binding template, or both. **← Profile rule**

Compliant ← Level of compliancy

A .NET Web service supports generating a WSDL 1.1 service description by using reflection on the **WebService** class. **← Comment**

Messaging

Messaging is the exchange of protocol elements, usually over a network. Messages encapsulate information transmitted to and from a Web service. These messages do not provide programming instructions; rather they specify to a Web services server which operations to invoke. According to the WS-I Basic Profile, the messaging system uses the following standards at the specified version levels:

- Simple Object Access Protocol (SOAP) 1.1 (*http://www.w3.org/TR/SOAP/*)
- Extensible Markup Language (XML) 1.0 (Second Edition) (*http://www.w3.org/TR/REC-xml*)
- RFC2616: Hypertext Transfer Protocol—HTTP/1.1 (*http://www.ietf.org/rfc/rfc2616*)
- RFC2965: HTTP State Management Mechanism (*http://www.ietf.org/rfc/rfc2965*)

XML Representation of SOAP Messages

This section includes the rules included in section 3.1 of the Basic Profile, which deals with the XML representation of SOAP messages. All these directives are based on the SOAP 1.1, Section 4 standard (*http://www.w3.org/TR/SOAP#_Toc478383494*).

R0001

An INSTANCE MUST be described by a WSDL 1.1 service description, by a UDDI binding template, or both.

Compliant

A .NET Web service automatically has built-in support for generating a WSDL 1.1 service description. If you invoke a .NET Web service using a normal HTTP GET request with a query string of ?WSDL, then it will use reflection on the **WebService** inherited class to generate a WSDL description.

R0002

A DESCRIPTION MAY contain conformance claims regarding instances, as specified in the conformance claim schema.

Unique

This is not mandatory. When a .NET Web service generates a WSDL description, it does not support including any conformance claims.

R0003

A DESCRIPTION's conformance claims MUST be children of the `wsdl:documentation` element of each of the elements: `wsdl:port`, `wsdl:binding`, `wsdl:portType`, `wsdl:operation` (as a child element of `wsdl:portType` but not of `wsdl:binding`) and `wsdl:message`.

Unique

When a .NET Web service generates a WSDL description, it does not support including any conformance claims.

R0004

A MESSAGE MAY contain conformance claims, as specified in the conformance claim schema.

Compliant

A .NET Web service properly handles a SOAP message that adheres to this rule.

R0005

A MESSAGE's conformance claims MUST be carried as SOAP header blocks.

Compliant

A .NET Web service properly handles a SOAP message that adheres to this rule.

R0006

A MESSAGE MAY contain conformance claims for more than one profile.

Compliant

A .NET Web service properly handles a SOAP message that adheres to this rule.

R0007

A SENDER MUST NOT use the `soap:mustUnderstand` attribute when sending a SOAP header block containing a conformance claim.

Compliant

A .NET Web service properly handles a SOAP message that adheres to this rule.

R3020

REGDATA of type `uddi:tModel` claiming conformance with a Profile MUST be categorized using the ws-i-org:conformsTo:2002_12 taxonomy.

Not applicable

The UDDI registration of a Web service is outside the scope of creating a Web service.

R3030

REGDATA of `type uddi:tModel` claiming conformance with a Profile MUST use the ws-i-org:conformsTo:2002_12 categorization value corresponding to the conformance claim URI for that Profile.

Not applicable

The UDDI registration of a Web service is outside the scope of creating a Web service.

R3021

A REGISTRY MUST support the WS-I Conformance category system by adding the ws-i-org:conformsTo:2002_12 tModel definition in its registry content.

Not applicable

The UDDI registration of a Web service is outside the scope of creating a Web service.

R3005

REGDATA other than `uddi:tModel` elements representing conformant Web service types MUST NOT be categorized using the ws-i-org:conformsTo:2002_12 taxonomy and a categorization of "http://ws-i.org/profiles/basic/1.0".

Not applicable

The UDDI registration of a Web service is outside the scope of creating a Web service.

R3004

REGDATA of type `uddi:tModel` MUST be constructed so that the conformance claim it makes is consistent with the conformance claim made by the `wsdl:binding` to which it refers.

Not applicable

The UDDI registration of a Web service is outside the scope of creating a Web service.

R4001

A RECEIVER MUST accept messages that include the Unicode Byte Order Mark (BOM).

Compliant

A .NET Web service properly handles a SOAP message that adheres to this rule. A .NET Web service will handle a SOAP message that either does or does not include the BOM, as well as either UTF-8 (Universal Transformation Format) or UTF-16 encoding.

R1000

When a MESSAGE contains a `soap:Fault` element, that element MUST NOT have element children other than `faultcode`, `faultstring`, `faultactor` and `detail`.

Typically Compliant

If, when an exception is thrown in a .NET Web service, the type of exception thrown does not inherit from the **SoapException** class, then the .NET runtime automatically wraps the exception in a **SoapException**. When serialized into a SOAP message, a **SoapException** only includes the **faultcode**, **faultstring**, **detail**, and, optionally, the **faultactor** elements. If you specify a **detail** parameter, you must make sure the main element is a **detail** element that contains your child nodes. Here is an example of how to do this:

```
XmlDocument doc = new XmlDocument();
// detail node is required to be the parent element
XmlNode detail = doc.CreateNode(XmlNodeType.Element, "detail", "");
detail.AppendChild(doc.CreateNode(XmlNodeType.Element, "MyElement", ""));
throw new SoapException("MyFault", SoapException.ServerFaultCode, "MyActor",
detail);
```

R1001

When a MESSAGE contains a `soap:Fault` element its element children MUST be unqualified.

Typically Compliant

If, when an exception is thrown in a Web service, the type of exception thrown does not inherit from the **SoapException** class, then the .NET runtime automatically wraps the exception in a **SoapException**. When serialized into a SOAP message, a **SoapException** does not qualify the element children of the **soap:Fault** element. If you specify a **detail** parameter, you must make sure not to specify a prefix for the main **detail** node. Here is an example illustrating what <u>not</u> to do:

```
XmlDocument doc = new XmlDocument();
// show incorrect specifying of a prefix for the detail node
XmlNode detail = doc.CreateNode(XmlNodeType.Element, "soap",  "detail",
"http://schemas.xmlsoap.org/soap/envelope/");
detail.AppendChild(doc.CreateNode(XmlNodeType.Element, "MyElement", ""));
throw new SoapException("MyFault", SoapException.ServerFaultCode, "MyActor",
detail);
```

R1002

A RECEIVER MUST accept fault messages that have any number of elements, including zero, appearing as children of the `detail` element. Such children can be qualified or unqualified.

Compliant

If you specify a **detail** parameter in the constructor of a **SoapException**, you can include child elements to the **detail** element but it is not required.

R1003

A RECEIVER MUST accept fault messages that have any number of qualified or unqualified attributes, including zero, appearing on the `detail` element. The namespace of qualified attributes can be anything other than "http://schemas.xmlsoap.org/soap/envelope/".

Typically Compliant

If you specify a **detail** parameter in the constructor of a **SoapException**, you can include attributes with the **detail** element, as long as the namespace specified is not "http://schemas.xmlsoap.org/soap/envelope/". Here is an example of what <u>not</u> to do:

```
XmlDocument doc = new XmlDocument();
XmlNode detail = doc.CreateNode(XmlNodeType.Element, "detail", "");
detail.Attributes.Append(doc.CreateAttribute("soap", "MyAttribute",
"http://schemas.xmlsoap.org/soap/envelope/"));
throw new SoapException("MyFault", SoapException.ServerFaultCode, "MyActor",
detail);
```

R1016

A RECEIVER MUST accept fault messages that carry an `xml:lang` attribute on the `faultstring` element.

Unique

The **SoapException** class does not support including an **xml:lang** attribute on the **faultstring** element in the SOAP response when an exception is thrown in a .NET Web service.

R1004

When a MESSAGE contains a `faultcode` element the content of that element SHOULD be one of the fault codes defined in SOAP 1.1 or a namespace qualified fault code.

Compliant

The **SoapException** class defines four constants that represent the four possible fault codes defined in SOAP 1.1. The constants are **ClientFaultCode**, **MustUnderstandFaultCode**, **ServerFaultCode**, and **VersionMismatchFaultCode**. Although it is not mandatory, you should pass one of these constants, or a namespace qualified fault code, as the code parameter of the constructor when you throw an exception. Here is an example using a SOAP 1.1 fault code:

```
throw new SoapException("MyFault", SoapException.ClientFaultCode);
```

R1031

When a MESSAGE contains a `faultcode` element the content of that element SHOULD NOT use the SOAP 1.1 "dot" notation to refine the meaning of the Fault.

Compliant

Although it is not mandatory, when you throw a **SoapException** exception, avoid passing an **XmlQualifiedName** with a name property set to one of the fault codes defined in SOAP 1.1 that has been appended with an additional value as the code parameter of the constructor. Here is an example of what to avoid:

```
string code = SoapException.ClientFaultCode.Name + ".Type";
throw new SoapException("My Fault", new XmlQualifiedName(code));
```

R1005

A MESSAGE MUST NOT contain `soap:encodingStyle` attributes on any of the elements whose namespace name is "http://schemas.xmlsoap.org/soap/envelope/".

Typically Compliant

To ensure that a .NET Web service does not require **soap:encodingStyle** attributes in the SOAP message, you must not use a **SoapRpcMethodAttribute** or **SoapRpcServiceAttribute**. Additionally, if the **SoapDocumentMethodAttribute** or **SoapDocumentServiceAttribute** is used, then the **Use** property must not be set to **SoapBindingUse.Encoded**.

R1006

A MESSAGE MUST NOT contain `soap:encodingStyle` attributes on any element that is a child of `soap:Body`.

Typically Compliant

To ensure that a .NET Web service does not require **soap:encodingStyle** attributes in the SOAP message, you must not use a **SoapRpcMethodAttribute** or **SoapRpcServiceAttribute**. Additionally, if the **SoapDocumentMethodAttribute** or **SoapDocumentServiceAttribute** is used, then the **Use** property must not be set to **SoapBindingUse.Encoded**.

R1007

A MESSAGE described in an rpc-literal binding MUST NOT contain `soap:encodingStyle` attribute on any elements are grandchildren of `soap:Body`.

Unique

A .NET Web service does not support an rpc-literal binding.

R1008

A MESSAGE MUST NOT contain a Document Type Declaration.

Compliant

A .NET Web service properly handles a SOAP message that adheres to this rule.

R1009

A MESSAGE MUST NOT contain Processing Instructions.

Compliant

A .NET Web service properly handles a SOAP message that adheres to this rule.

R1010

A RECEIVER MUST accept messages that contain an XML Declaration.

Compliant

A .NET Web service properly handles a SOAP message that adheres to this rule.

R1011

A MESSAGE MUST NOT have any element children of `soap:Envelope` following the `soap:Body` element.

Compliant

A .NET Web service properly handles a SOAP message that adheres to this rule.

R1012

A MESSAGE MUST be serialized as either UTF-8 or UTF-16.

Compliant

A .NET Web service properly handles a SOAP message serialized using either UTF-8 or UTF-16 encoding.

R1018

The media type of a MESSAGE's envelope MUST indicate the correct character encoding, using the charset parameter.

Compliant

A .NET Web service properly handles a message that adheres to this rule.

R1013

A MESSAGE containing a `soap:mustUnderstand` attribute MUST only use the lexical forms "0" and "1".

Compliant

A .NET Web service properly handles a SOAP message that adheres to this rule.

R1014

The children of the `soap:Body` element in a MESSAGE MUST be namespace qualified.

Compliant

A .NET Web service properly handles a SOAP message that adheres to this rule.

R1015

A RECEIVER MUST generate a fault if they encounter a message whose document element has a local name of "Envelope" but a namespace name that is not "http://schemas.xmlsoap.org/soap/envelope/".

Compliant

If a .NET Web service receives a message whose **Envelope** element has a namespace other then "http://schemas.xmlsoap.org/soap/envelope/" it returns a SOAP fault with a **faultstring** stating there is a possible SOAP version mismatch.

R1017

A RECEIVER MUST NOT mandate the use of the `xsi:type` attribute in messages except as required in order to indicate a derived type (see XML Schema Part 1: Structures, Section 2.6.1).

Compliant

A .NET Web service does not require that any elements in the request message assert their types using the **xsi:type** attribute. The element values sent in a request message are parsed and validated against the expected parameter type and a SOAP fault is returned if the value cannot be parsed.

The Soap Processing Model

This portion includes directives in section 3.2 of the basic profile, which alludes to information in SOAP 1.1, Section 2 (*http://www.w3.org/TR/SOAP#_Toc478383491*). SOAP 1.1, Section 2 defines a model for processing messages.

R1025

A RECEIVER MUST handle messages in such a way that it appears that all checking of mandatory headers is performed before any actual processing.

Potentially Compliant

A .NET Web service normally executes completely before checking if the mandatory headers were properly processed. If they were not, it returns a SOAP fault. The Web service determines whether a mandatory header is understood if either there is a **SoapHeaderAttribute** declared for the header or if the **DidUnderstand** property of the header is set to **true**. The following code demonstrates how to verify mandatory headers at the beginning of execution:

```
public MyHeaderType myHeader;
public SoapUnknownHeader[] unknownHeaders;

[WebMethod]
[SoapHeader("myHeader", Required=false)]
[SoapHeader("unknownHeaders", Required=false)]
public string HelloWorld()
{
    bool headersValid = true;

        // Check if known (declared) header
// is marked as mandatory
        if (myHeader.MustUnderstand == true)
        {
```

(continued)

(continued)

```
            // Validate the information in the
// known (declared) header
            if ((validation test of myHeader data) == false)
            {
                myHeader.DidUnderstand = false;
                headersValid = false;
            }
        }
        // Check for unknown headers marked as mandatory
        foreach (SoapUnknownHeader header in unknownHeaders)
        {
            if (header.MustUnderstand)
            {
                header.DidUnderstand = false;
                headersValid = false;
            }
        }
        if (headersValid == false)
        {
            // return before processing
            return null;
        }
        // Execute normal Web service processing here
}
```

R1027

A RECEIVER MUST generate a "soap:MustUnderstand" fault when a message contains a mandatory header block (i.e., one that has a `soap:mustUnderstand` attribute with the value "1") targeted at the receiver (via `soap:actor`) that the receiver does not understand.

Compliant

A .NET Web service automatically generates a **soap:MustUnderstand** fault if the **DidUnderstand** property is **false** on any header that has a **MustUnderstand** property value of **true**.

R1028

When a Fault is generated by a RECEIVER, further processing SHOULD NOT be performed on the SOAP message aside from that which is necessary to rollback, or compensate for, any effects of processing the message prior to the generation of the Fault.

Compliant

Although it is not mandatory, when an exception is thrown in a .NET Web service it will automatically stop processing and execute any exception management code.

R1029

Where the normal outcome of processing a SOAP message would have resulted in the transmission of a SOAP response, but rather a SOAP Fault is generated instead, a RECEIVER MUST transmit a SOAP Fault message in place of the response.

Compliant

A .NET Web service returns a SOAP fault message when an exception is thrown.

R1030

A RECEIVER that generates a SOAP Fault SHOULD notify the end user that a SOAP Fault has been generated when practical, by whatever means is deemed appropriate to the circumstance.

Compliant

Although it is not mandatory, when a .NET Web service fails, the end user that initiated the activity that triggered calling the Web service should be notified of the failure.

Using SOAP in HTTP

This portion includes directives in section 3.3 of the Basic Profile, which alludes to information in the following specifications:

- SOAP 1.1, Section 6 (*http://www.w3.org/TR/SOAP#_Toc478383526*)
- HTTP/1.1 (*http://www.ietf.org/rfc/rfc2616*)
- HTTP State Management Mechanism (*http://www.ietf.org/rfc/rfc2965*)

SOAP 1.1 defines a single protocol binding, which is for HTTP and the profile mandates the use of that binding.

HTTP/1.1 has several performance advantages and is more clearly specified in comparison to HTTP/1.0. Note that support for HTTP/1.0 is implied in HTTP/1.1, and that intermediaries may change the version of a message; for more information about HTTP versioning, see RFC2145.

R1140

A MESSAGE SHOULD be sent using HTTP/1.1.

Compliant

A .NET Web service properly handles a message sent using HTTP/1.1.

R1141

A MESSAGE MUST be sent using either HTTP/1.1 or HTTP/1.0.

Compliant

A .NET Web service properly handles a message sent using either HTTP/1.1 or HTTP/1.0.

R1107

A RECEIVER MUST interpret SOAP messages containing only a `soap:Fault` element as a Fault.

Not Applicable

This rule is not applicable to creating a Web service.

R1132

A HTTP request MESSAGE MUST use the HTTP POST method.

Compliant

A .NET Web service properly handles a request that adheres to this rule.

R1108

A MESSAGE MUST NOT use the HTTP Extension Framework (RFC2774).

Compliant

A .NET Web service properly handles a request that adheres to this rule.

R1109

The value of the `SOAPAction` HTTP header field in a HTTP request MESSAGE MUST be a quoted string.

Compliant

A .NET Web service properly handles a request that adheres to this rule.

R1119

A RECEIVER MAY respond with a Fault if the value of the `SOAPAction` HTTP header field is not quoted.

Compliant

A .NET Web service does not respond with a Fault if the value of the **SOAPAction** HTTP header field is not quoted. Instead, it interprets the value exactly as if it were quoted.

R1110

An INSTANCE MAY accept connections on TCP port 80 (HTTP).

Compliant

The TCP port that a .NET Web service responds to depends on the IIS (Internet Information Server) configuration settings. By default, IIS uses port 80 but you can change it to any valid TCP port.

R1124

An INSTANCE MUST use a 2xx HTTP status code for responses that indicate a successful outcome of a request.

Compliant

This is the default behavior of a .NET Web service.

R1111

An INSTANCE SHOULD use a "200 OK" HTTP status code for responses that contain a SOAP message that is not a SOAP fault.

Compliant

This is the default behavior of a .NET Web service.

R1112

An INSTANCE SHOULD use either a "200 OK" or "202 Accepted" HTTP status code for a response that does do not contain a SOAP message but indicates successful HTTP outcome of a request.

Compliant

A .NET Web service returns a "202 Accepted" HTTP status code for a response that does not include a SOAP message. In the case of a one-way method, a SOAP message is not returned, as shown in the following example:

```
[WebMethod]
[SoapDocumentMethod(OneWay=true)]
public void Submit(string parameter)
{
  // Some action that does not require giving
  // any kind of response to caller
}
```

R1130

An INSTANCE MUST use HTTP status code "307 Temporary Redirect" when redirecting a request to a different endpoint.

Potentially Compliant

To redirect a request in a .NET Web service, you must explicitly set the HTTP status code and add a **Location** HTTP header. Using the **Response.Redirect** method won't return the correct status code. Here's an example of how to do this:

```
[WebMethod]
public string HelloWorld()
{
  Context.Response.StatusCode = 307;
  Context.Response.AddHeader("Location","<redirect URL>");
  return null;
}
```

R1131

A CONSUMER MAY automatically redirect a request when it encounters a "307 Temporary Redirect" HTTP status code in a response.

Not Applicable

This rule is not applicable to creating a Web service.

R1125

An INSTANCE MUST use a 4xx HTTP status code for responses that indicate a problem with the format of the request.

Unique

The default behavior of a .NET Web service is to return a 500 HTTP status code on any error result.

R1113

An INSTANCE SHOULD use a "400 Bad Request" HTTP status code, if the request message is a malformed HTTP request, or not well-formed XML.

Compliant

This is not mandatory. The default behavior of a .NET Web service is to return a 500 HTTP status code on any error result.

R1114

An INSTANCE SHOULD use a "405 Method not Allowed" HTTP status code if the request method was not "POST".

Compliant

This is not mandatory. The default behavior of a .NET Web service is to return a 500 HTTP status code on any error result. Also, the default behavior of a .NET Web service for an HTTP GET request returns information about the Web service.

R1115

An INSTANCE SHOULD use a "415 Unsupported Media Type" HTTP status code if the Content-Type HTTP request header did not have a value consistent with the value specified for the corresponding binding of the input message.

Compliant

This is not mandatory. The default behavior of a .NET Web service is to return a 500 HTTP status code on any error result.

R1126

An INSTANCE MUST use a "500 Internal Server Error" HTTP status code if the response message is a SOAP Fault.

Compliant

When an exception is thrown in a .NET Web service, it generates a SOAP fault as the response and sets the HTTP status code to "500 Internal Server Error."

R1120

An INSTANCE MAY use the HTTP state mechanism ("Cookies").

Compliant

You can access the cookies collection in a Web service request with the **Context** property inherited from the **WebService** base class. The following example shows how to read a cookie using the **Request** property and how to return a cookie using the **Response** property:

```
[WebMethod]
public string HelloWorld()
{
 // Access a cookie passed in on the request
 HttpCookie myCookie = Context.Request.Cookies.Get("MyCookie");

 // Add a new cookie to be sent back in the response
 Context.Response.Cookies.Add(new HttpCookie("NewCookie","value"));

 return "Hello World";
}
```

R1122

An INSTANCE using Cookies SHOULD conform to RFC2965.

Compliant

The cookies support in a .NET Web service conforms to RFC2965.

R1121

An INSTANCE SHOULD NOT require consumer support for Cookies in order to function correctly.

Compliant

Although it is not mandatory, cookies should only be used to provide hints for such things as optimization and not to ensure that the Web service functions correctly.

R1123

The value of the cookie MUST be considered to be opaque by the CONSUMER.

Not Applicable

This rule is not applicable to creating a Web service.

Service Description

This portion includes directives in section 4 of the Basic Profile, which alludes to information in the following specifications:

- WSDL 1.1 (*http://www.w3.org/TR/wsdl.html*)
- XML Schema Part 1: Structures (*http://www.w3.org/TR/xmlschema-1*)
- XML Schema Part 2: Datatypes (*http://www.w3.org/TR/xmlschema-2*)

The WSDL specification describes and publishes the formats and protocols of a Web service in a standard way. WSDL elements contain a description of the data, usually in XML, that is passed to the Web service so that both the sender and the receiver understand the data being exchanged. The WSDL elements also contain a description of the operations to be performed on that data so that the receiver of the message knows how to process it, and a binding to a protocol or a transport, so that the sender knows how to send it. Typically, WSDL is used with SOAP, and the WSDL specification includes a SOAP binding.

XML provides the description, storage, and transmission format for data exchanged via a Web service. XML elements and attributes define type and structure information for the data they carry. The XML syntax specifies how data is generically represented, defines how and with what qualities of service the data is transmitted, and details how the services are published and discovered.

Document Structure

This portion includes directives in section 4.2 of the Basic Profile, which alludes to information in WSDL 1.1 (*http://www.w3.org/TR/wsdl.html*). This defines an XML-based structure for describing Web services.

R2028

A DESCRIPTION using the WSDL namespace (prefixed "wsdl" in this Profile) MUST be valid according to the XML Schema found at "http://schemas.xmlsoap.org/wsdl/2003-02-11.xsd".

Compliant

A WSDL description generated by a .NET Web service adheres to this rule.

R2029

A DESCRIPTION using the WSDL SOAP binding namespace (prefixed "soapbind" in this Profile) MUST be valid according to the XML Schema found at "http://schemas.xmlsoap.org/wsdl/soap/2003-02-11.xsd".

Compliant

A WSDL description generated by a .NET Web service adheres to this rule.

R2001

A DESCRIPTION MUST only use the WSDL "import" statement to import another WSDL description.

Compliant

A WSDL description generated by a .NET Web service adheres to this rule. A WSDL import statement is created if you declare and use an additional binding with a **WebServiceBindingAttribute**. When a WSDL description is generated for the following example, it will include a WSDL import statement that imports the WSDL description "http://www.contoso.com/MySevice.asmx?wsdl":

```
[WebService]
[WebServiceBinding(Name="RemoteBinding",
  Namespace="http://www.contoso.com/MyBinding",
  Location="http://www.contoso.com/MyService.asmx?WSDL")]
public class MyService
{
  [WebMethod]
  [SoapDocumentMethod(Binding="RemoteBinding")]
  public string HelloWorld()
  {
    return "Hello World";
  }
}
```

R2002

To import XML Schema Definitions, a DESCRIPTION MUST use the XML Schema "import" statement.

Typically Compliant

If you use a **WebServiceBindingAttribute** and do not specify the **Location** property or set the **Location** property to empty, it causes a WSDL import statement to be created for importing an XML Schema Definition. Here's an example of what not to do:

```
[WebService]
[WebServiceBinding(Name="RemoteBinding",
  Namespace="http://www.contoso.com/MyBinding",
  Location="")]
public class MyService
{
  [WebMethod]
  [SoapDocumentMethod(Binding="RemoteBinding")]
  public string HelloWorld()
  {
    return "Hello World";
  }
}
```

R2003

A DESCRIPTION MUST use the XML Schema "import" statement only within the `xsd:schema` element of the types section.

Compliant

A WSDL description generated by a .NET Web service adheres to this rule. A .NET Web service will not create an XML Schema "import" statement to import an externally defined XML Schema, but will create them for importing into the primary XML Schema definition the namespace of additional schemas defined within the types section.

R2004

A DESCRIPTION MUST NOT use the XML Schema "import" statement to import a Schema from any document whose root element is not "schema" from the namespace "http://www.w3.org/2001/XMLSchema".

Compliant

A WSDL description generated by a .NET Web service adheres to this rule. A .NET Web service will not create an XML Schema "import" statement to import an externally defined XML Schema, but will create them for importing into the primary XML Schema definition the namespace of additional schemas defined within the types section.

R2009

An XML Schema directly or indirectly imported by a DESCRIPTION MAY include the Unicode Byte Order Mark (BOM).

Compliant

A WSDL description generated by a .NET Web service adheres to this rule. A .NET Web service will not include an XML Schema "import" statement for importing an externally defined schema.

R2010

An XML Schema directly or indirectly imported by a DESCRIPTION MUST use either UTF-8 or UTF-16 encoding.

Compliant

A WSDL description generated by a .NET Web service adheres to this rule. A .NET Web service will not include an XML Schema "import" statement for importing an externally defined schema.

R2011

An XML Schema directly or indirectly imported by a DESCRIPTION MUST use version 1.0 of the eXtensible Markup Language W3C Recommendation.

Compliant

A WSDL description generated by a .NET Web service adheres to this rule. A .NET Web service will not include an XML Schema "import" statement for importing an externally defined schema.

R2007

A DESCRIPTION MUST specify a non-empty location attribute on the `wsdl:import` element.

Compliant

A WSDL description generated by a .NET Web service adheres to this rule.

R2008

In a DESCRIPTION the value of the location attribute of a `wsdl:import` element SHOULD be treated as a hint.

Not Applicable

This rule is not applicable to creating a Web service.

R2022

When they appear in a DESCRIPTION, `wsdl:import` elements MUST precede all other elements from the WSDL namespace except `wsdl:documentation`.

Compliant

A WSDL description generated by a .NET Web service adheres to this rule.

R2023

When they appear in a DESCRIPTION, `wsdl:types` elements MUST precede all other elements from the WSDL namespace except `wsdl:documentation` and `wsdl:import`.

Compliant

A WSDL description generated by a .NET Web service adheres to this rule.

R4004

A DESCRIPTION MUST use version 1.0 of the eXtensible Markup Language W3C Recommendation.

Compliant

A WSDL description generated by a .NET Web service adheres to this rule.

R4002

A DESCRIPTION MAY include the Unicode Byte Order Mark (BOM).

Compliant

A WSDL description generated by a .NET Web service does not include a BOM.

R4003

A DESCRIPTION MUST use either UTF-8 or UTF-16 encoding.

Compliant

A WSDL description generated by a .NET Web service uses UTF-8 encoding.

R2005

The `targetNamespace` attribute on the `wsdl:definitions` element of a description that is being imported MUST have same the value as the `namespace` attribute on the `wsdl:import` element in the importing DESCRIPTION.

Typically Compliant

A WSDL description generated by a .NET Web service includes a **wsdl:import** element when you use the **WebServiceBindingAttribute**. In this case, you must make sure to specify a value for the **Namespace** property and also ensure that the value matches the **targetNamespace** attribute on the **wsdl:definitions** element of the WSDL description specified by the **Location** property.

R2020

The `wsdl:documentation` element MAY occur as a child of the `wsdl:import` element in a DESCRIPTION.

Compliant

A WSDL description generated by a .NET Web service does not include a **wsdl:documentation** element as a child of a **wsdl:import** element.

R2021

The `wsdl:documentation` element MAY occur as a child of the `wsdl:part` element in a DESCRIPTION.

Compliant

A WSDL description generated by a .NET Web service does not include a **wsdl:documentation** element as a child of a **wsdl:part** element.

R2024

The `wsdl:documentation` element MAY occur as a first child of the `wsdl:definitions` element in a DESCRIPTION.

Compliant

A WSDL description generated by a .NET Web service does not include a **wsdl:documentation** element as a child of a **wsdl:definitions** element.

R2025

A DESCRIPTION containing WSDL extensions MUST NOT use them to contradict other requirements of the Profile.

Compliant

A WSDL description generated by a .NET Web service adheres to this rule.

R2026

A DESCRIPTION SHOULD NOT include extension elements with a `wsdl:required` attribute value of "true" on any WSDL construct (`wsdl:binding`, `wsdl:portType`, `wsdl:message`, `wsdl:types`, or `wsdl:import`) that claims conformance to the Profile.

Compliant

Although it is not mandatory, a WSDL Description generated by a .NET Web service does not include any extension elements with a **wsdl:required** attribute value of **true**.

R2027

If during the processing of an element in the WSDL namespace in a description, a consumer encounters a WSDL extension element amongst its element children, that has a `wsdl:required` attribute with a boolean value of "true" that the consumer does not understand or cannot process, the CONSUMER MUST fail processing of that element in the WSDL namespace.

Not Applicable

This rule is not applicable to creating a Web service.

Types

This portion of the profile modifies and refers to WSDL 1.1, Section 2.2 (*http://www.w3.org/TR/wsdl#_types*), which describes WSDL data types.

R2101

A DESCRIPTION MUST NOT use QName references to elements in namespaces that have been neither imported, nor defined in the referring WSDL document.

Compliant

A WSDL description generated by a .NET Web service adheres to this rule.

R2102

A QName reference to a Schema component in a DESCRIPTION MUST use the namespace defined in the `targetNamespace` attribute on the `xsd:schema` element, or to a namespace defined in the `namespace` attribute on an `xsd:import` element within the `xsd:schema` element.

Compliant

A WSDL description generated by a .NET Web service adheres to this rule.

R2105

All `xsd:schema` elements contained in a `wsdl:types` element of a DESCRIPTION MUST have a `targetNamespace` attribute with a valid and non-null value, UNLESS the `xsd:schema` element has `xsd:import` and/or `xsd:annotation` as its only child element(s).

Compliant

A WSDL description generated by a .NET Web service adheres to this rule. A .NET Web service generates one **xsd:schema** element for each namespace specified for parameters, return values, or headers. The following example generates three **xsd:schema** elements with the specified namespaces in the WSDL:

```
[WebService(Namespace="MyNamespace1")]
public class MyService : System.Web.Services.WebService
{
  [WebMethod]
  [return: XmlElement(Namespace="MyNamespace2")]
  public string HelloWorld([XmlElement(Namespace="MyNamespace3")] string param1)
  {
   return "Hello World";
  }
}
```

R2110

In a DESCRIPTION, `array` declarations MUST NOT extend or restrict the `soapenc:Array` type.

Compliant

A WSDL description generated by a .NET Web service adheres to this rule.

R2111

In a DESCRIPTION, `array` declarations MUST NOT use `wsdl:arrayType` attribute in the type declaration.

Compliant

A WSDL description generated by a .NET Web service adheres to this rule.

R2112

In a DESCRIPTION, `array` declaration wrapper elements SHOULD NOT be named using the convention ArrayOfXXX.

Compliant

This is not mandatory. A WSDL description generated by a .NET Web service names the **xsd:complexType** element as ArrayOfXXX in an array declaration.

R2113

A MESSAGE containing serialized arrays MUST NOT include the `soapenc:arrayType` attribute.

Compliant

A .NET Web service properly handles a SOAP message that adheres to this rule.

R2114

The target namespace for WSDL definitions and the target namespace for schema definitions in a DESCRIPTION MAY be the same.

Compliant

A WSDL description generated by a .NET Web service typically uses the namespace specified in the **Namespace** property of the **WebServiceAttribute** for both the WSDL definition and any schema definitions. The exception is if you specifically declare the namespace for a parameter or return value of a Web method by using **XmlElementAttribute**, **XmlTypeAttribute**, or a similar method.

Messages

This portion of the profile modifies and refers to WSDL 1.1, Section 2.3 (*http://www.w3.org/TR/wsdl#_messages*), which describes WSDL messages. A WSDL message is an abstract definition of the data, in the form of a message presented either as an entire document or as arguments to be mapped to a method invocation.

R2201

A document-literal binding in a DESCRIPTION MUST, in each of its `soapbind:body` element(s), have at most one part listed in the `parts` attribute, if the `parts` attribute is specified.

Compliant

A WSDL description generated by a .NET Web service does not specify a **parts** attribute on the **soapbind:body** element(s).

R2210

If a document-literal binding in a DESCRIPTION does not specify the `parts` attribute on a `soapbind:body` element, the corresponding abstract `wsdl:message` MUST define zero or one `wsdl:parts`.

Typically Compliant

A WSDL description generated by a .NET Web service typically defines a single **wsdl:part** for a **wsdl:message** when using document-literal binding. The exception is if you use a **SoapDocumentServiceAttribute** or **SoapDocumentMethodAttribute** specifying the **ParameterStyle** property with a value of **SoapParameterStyle.Bare**, in which case it includes one **wsdl:part** for each parameter defined. When using **SoapParameterStyle.Bare** you must only have zero or one parameters. Here is an example of what not to do:

```
[WebMethod]
[SoapDocumentMethod(ParameterStyle=SoapParameterStyle.Bare)]
public string HelloWorld(string param1, string param2)
{
  return "Hello World";
}
```

R2202

A `wsdl:binding` in a DESCRIPTION MAY contain `soapbind:body` element(s) that specify that zero parts form the `soap:body`.

Compliant

A WSDL description generated by a .NET Web service does not specify a **parts** attribute on the **soapbind:body** element(s).

R2203

An rpc-literal binding in a DESCRIPTION MUST refer, in its `soapbind:body` element(s), only to `wsdl:part` element(s) that have been defined using the `type` attribute.

Unique

A .NET Web service does not support generating a WSDL description with an rpc-literal binding.

R2211

A MESSAGE described with an rpc-literal binding MUST NOT have the `xsi:nil` attribute with a value of "1" or "true" on the part accessors.

Unique

A .NET Web service does not support generating a WSDL description with an rpc-literal binding.

R2207

A `wsdl:message` in a DESCRIPTION MAY contain `wsdl:parts` that use the `elements` attribute provided those `wsdl:parts` are not referred to by a `soapbind:body` in an rpc-literal binding.

Compliant

A WSDL description generated by a .NET Web service adheres to this rule. A .NET Web service uses the elements attribute for all **wsdl:part**s defined in a **wsdl:message**, and only uses document-literal bindings.

R2204

A document-literal binding in a DESCRIPTION MUST refer, in each of its `soapbind:body` element(s), only to `wsdl:part` element(s) that have been defined using the `element` attribute.

Compliant

A WSDL description generated by a .NET Web service adheres to this rule.

R2208

A binding in a DESCRIPTION MAY contain `soapbind:header` element(s) that refer to `wsdl:parts` in the same `wsdl:message` that are referred to by its `soapbind:body` element(s).

Compliant

A WSDL description generated by a .NET Web service adheres to this rule. If a **Webmethod** has a **SoapHeaderAttribute** specified, then it generates a **soapbind:header** element and a separate **wsdl:message** from the **wsdl:message** created to define the **wsdl:parts** for the **soapbind:body**.

R2205

A `wsdl:binding` in a DESCRIPTION MUST refer, in each of its `soapbind:header`, `soapbind:headerfault` and `soapbind:fault` elements, only to `wsdl:part` element(s) that have been defined using the `element` attribute.

Compliant

When a .NET Web service generates a WSDL description, it does not create **soapbind:headerfault** or **soapbind:fault** elements. If a **Webmethod** has a **SoapHeaderAttribute** specified, then it generates a **soapbind:header** element and a **wsdl:message** element specifically for the header that contains **wsdl:part**s defined using the element attribute.

R2209

A `wsdl:binding` in a DESCRIPTION SHOULD bind every `wsdl:part` of a `wsdl:message` in the `wsdl:portType` to which it refers to one of `soapbind:body`, `soapbind:header`, `soapbind:fault` or `soapbind:headerfault`.

Compliant

Although it is not mandatory, a WSDL description generated by a .NET Web service defines only the **wsdl:input** and **wsdl:output** elements for a **wsdl:operation** in a **wsdl:portType** element. It also implicitly binds every part of a **wsdl:message** in that **wsdl:portType** by omitting a **part**s attribute on the **soapbind:body** element.

R2206

A `wsdl:message` in a DESCRIPTION containing a `wsdl:part` that uses the `element` attribute MUST refer, in that attribute, to a global element declaration.

Compliant

A WSDL description generated by a .NET Web service adheres to this rule.

Port Types

A WSDL port type is an abstract set of operations mapped to one or more end points, defining the collection of operations for a binding; the collection of operations, because it is abstract, can be mapped to multiple transports through various bindings.

R2301

The order of the elements in the `soap:body` of a MESSAGE MUST be the same as that of the `wsdl:parts` in the `wsdl:message` that describes it.

Compliant

A .NET Web service properly handles a SOAP message that adheres to this rule.

R2302

A DESCRIPTION MAY use the `parameterOrder` attribute of an `wsdl:operation` element to indicate the return value and method signatures as a hint to code generators.

Compliant

A WSDL description generated by a .NET Web service does not use the **parameterOrder** attribute on any **wsdl:operation** elements.

R2303

A DESCRIPTION MUST NOT use Solicit-Response and Notification type operations in a `wsdl:portType` definition.

Compliant

A WSDL description generated by a .NET Web service adheres to this rule.

R2304

A `wsdl:portType` in a DESCRIPTION MUST have operations with distinct values for their `name` attributes.

Compliant

If there are multiple **WebMethods** defined with the same name (that is, they are overloaded), the .NET Web service fails with an exception when it tries to generate the WSDL description. In the case of overloaded **WebMethods**, you must use the **MessageName** property of the **WebMethod** attribute to specify a distinct value that will be used as the operation name in the WSDL. Here is an example:

```
[WebMethod]
public string HelloWorld()
{
  return "Hello World";
}

[WebMethod(MessageName="HelloWorldMsg")]
public string HelloWorld(string msg)
{
  return "Hello World - " + msg;
}
```

R2305

A `wsdl:portType` in a DESCRIPTION MUST be constructed so that the `parameterOrder` attribute, if present, omits at most 1 `wsdl:part` from the output message.

Compliant

A WSDL description generated by a .NET Web service does not use the **parameterOrder** attribute.

R2306

A `wsdl:message` in a DESCRIPTION MUST NOT specify both `type` and `element` attributes on the same `wsdl:part`.

Compliant

A WSDL description generated by a .NET Web service adheres to this rule. When it generates a WSDL description, a .NET Web service uses the **element** attribute on a **wsdl:part** element.

Bindings

A WSDL binding is the concrete protocol and data formats for the operations and messages defined for a particular port type.

R2401

A `wsdl:binding` element in a DESCRIPTION MUST use WSDL SOAP Binding as defined in WSDL 1.1 Section 3.

Compliant

A WSDL description generated by a .NET Web service adheres to this rule.

SOAP Binding

SOAP is the most popular transport for WSDL. The SOAP specification contains predefined rules for physically representing such data types as Booleans, integers, and arrays. Binding to SOAP therefore requires the abstract data types, messages, and operations to be bound to concrete physical representations on the wire.

R2701

The `wsdl:binding` element in a DESCRIPTION MUST be constructed so that its `soapbind:binding` child element specifies the `transport` attribute.

Compliant

A WSDL description generated by a .NET Web service adheres to this rule.

R2702

A `wsdl:binding` in a DESCRIPTION MUST specify the HTTP transport protocol with SOAP binding. Specifically, the `transport` attribute of is `soapbind:binding` child MUST have the value "http://schemas.xmlsoap.org/soap/http".

Compliant

A WSDL description generated by a .NET Web service adheres to this rule.

R2705

A `wsdl:binding` in a DESCRIPTION MUST use either be a rpc-literal binding or a document-literal binding.

Typically Compliant

By default, a WSDL description generated by a .NET Web service uses the "document" value for the style attribute. You must not use a **SoapRpcMethodAttribute** or **SoapRpcServiceAttribute**. If you do use a **SoapRpcServiceAttribute** but not any **SoapDocumentMethodAttributes**, or instead, use a **SoapRpcMethodAttribute** for all of your **Webmethods**, then you will be compliant with this rule but non-compliant with other rules.

R2706

A `wsdl:binding` in a DESCRIPTION MUST use the value of "literal" for the `use` attribute in all `soapbind:body`, `soapbind:fault`, `soapbind:header`, and `soapbind:headerfault` elements.

Typically Compliant

By default, a WSDL description generated by a .NET Web service uses the "literal" value for the **use** attribute on all **soapbind:body** and **soapbind:header** elements, and does not generate **soapbind:headerfault** elements. You must not use a **SoapRpcMethodAttribute** or **SoapRpcServiceAttribute**. If instead, you use either a **SoapDocumentMethodAttribute** or **SoapDocumentServiceAttribute** then you must not set the **Use** property to **SoapBindingUse.Encoded**.

R2707

A `wsdl:binding` in a DESCRIPTION that contains one or more `soapbind:body`, `soapbind:fault`, `soapbind:header`, or `soapbind:headerfault` elements that do not specify the `use` attribute MUST be interpreted as though the value "literal" had been specified in each case.

Not Applicable

This rule is not applicable to creating a Web service. A WSDL description generated by a .NET Web service always includes the **use** attribute for **soapbind:body** and **soapbind:header** elements, and does create **soapbind:headerfault** elements.

R2709

A `wsdl:portType` in a DESCRIPTION MAY have zero or more `wsdl:bindings` that refer to it, defined in the same or other WSDL documents.

Compliant

A WSDL description generated by a .NET Web service adheres to this rule.

R2710

The operations in a `wsdl:binding` in a DESCRIPTION MUST result in wire signatures that are different from one another.

Typically Compliant

By default a WSDL description generated by a .NET Web service will have a wrapper element of the same name as the **Webmethod** to ensure the wire signature is unique. However, if you use a **SoapDocumentMethodAttribute** and set the **ParameterStyle** property to **SoapParameterStyle.Bare**, then you must ensure the parameters of your **Webmethod** are not identical to the parameters of any other **Webmethod** in your Web service.

R2711

A DESCRIPTION SHOULD NOT have more than one `wsdl:port` with the same value for the `location` attribute of the `soapbind:address` element.

Compliant

Although it is not mandatory, a WSDL description generated by a .NET Web service adheres to this rule.

R2712

A document-literal binding MUST be represented on the wire as a MESSAGE with a `soap:Body` whose child element is an instance of the global element declaration referenced by the corresponding `wsdl:message part`.

Compliant

A .NET Web service properly handles a SOAP message that adheres to this rule.

R2714

For one-way operations, an INSTANCE MUST NOT return a HTTP response that contains a SOAP envelope. Specifically, the HTTP response entity-body must be empty.

Compliant

A .NET Web service returns an empty HTTP response body for a **Webmethod** that is marked as one-way by using a **SoapDocumentMethodAttribute** with the **OneWay** property set to **true**. Here is an example:

```
[WebMethod]
[SoapDocumentMethod(OneWay=true)]
public void HelloWorld()
{
  // Some processing
}
```

R2750

A CONSUMER MUST ignore SOAP response carried in a response from a one-way operation.

Not Applicable

This rule is not applicable to creating a Web service. A .NET Web service does not return a SOAP response for a one-way operation.

R2727

For one-way operations, a CONSUMER MUST NOT interpret a successful HTTP response status code (i.e., 2xx) to mean the message is valid or that the receiver would process it.

Not Applicable

This rule is not applicable to creating a Web service. A .NET Web service always returns a "202 Accepted" HTTP response for a one-way operation, even if an exception is thrown in that operation.

R2716

A document-literal binding in a DESCRIPTION MUST NOT have the `namespace` attribute specified on contained `soapbind:body`, `soapbind:header`, `soapbind:headerfault` and `soapbind:fault` elements.

Compliant

A WSDL description generated by a .NET Web service adheres to this rule.

R2717

An rpc-literal binding in a DESCRIPTION MUST have the `namespace` attribute specified, the value of which MUST be an absolute URI, on contained `soapbind:body` elements.

Unique

A .NET Web service does not support generating a WSDL description with an rpc-literal binding.

R2726

An rpc-literal binding in a DESCRIPTION MUST NOT have the `namespace` attribute specified on contained `soapbind:header`, `soapbind:headerfault` and `soapbind:fault` elements.

Unique

A .NET Web service does not support generating a WSDL description with an rpc-literal binding.

R2718

A `wsdl:binding` in a DESCRIPTION MUST have the same set of `wsdl:operations` as the `wsdl:portType` to which it refers.

Compliant

A WSDL description generated by a .NET Web service adheres to this rule.

R2719

A `wsdl:binding` in a DESCRIPTION MAY contain no `soapbind:headerfault` elements if there are no known header faults.

Compliant

A WSDL description generated by a .NET Web service does not contain any **soapbind:headerfault** elements.

R2740

A `wsdl:binding` in a DESCRIPTION SHOULD contain a `soapbind:fault` describing each known fault.

Compliant

This is not mandatory. A WSDL description generated by a .NET Web service does not include **soapbind:fault** elements.

R2741

A `wsdl:binding` in a DESCRIPTION SHOULD contain a `soapbind:headerfault` describing each known header fault.

Compliant

This is not mandatory. A WSDL description generated by a .NET Web service does not include **soapbind:headerfault** elements.

R2742

A MESSAGE MAY contain a fault detail entry in a SOAP fault that is not described by a `wsdl:fault` element in the corresponding WSDL description.

Compliant

Because a WSDL description generated by a .NET Web service does not include **wsdl:fault** elements, any SOAP message returned containing a **soap:Fault** element is not described by the WSDL description.

R2743

A MESSAGE MAY contain the details of a header processing related fault in a SOAP header block that is not described by a `wsdl:headerfault` element in the corresponding WSDL description.

Compliant

A WSDL description generated by a .NET Web service does not contain **wsdl:headerfault** elements, but you can return fault detail elements in the SOAP header block by including a **SoapHeaderAttribute** with the **Direction** property set to **SoapHeaderDirection.Fault**.

R2720

A `wsdl:binding` in a DESCRIPTION MUST use the attribute named `part` with a schema type of "NMTOKEN" on all contained `soapbind:header` and `soapbind:headerfault` elements.

Compliant

A WSDL description generated by a .NET Web service adheres to this rule.

R2749

A `wsdl:binding` in a DESCRIPTION MUST NOT use the attribute named parts on contained `soapbind:header` and `soapbind:headerfault` elements.

Compliant

A WSDL description generated by a .NET Web service adheres to this rule.

R2721

A `wsdl:binding` in a DESCRIPTION MUST have the `name` attribute specified on all contained `soapbind:fault` elements.

Compliant

A WSDL description generated by a .NET Web service does not contain any **soapbind:fault** elements.

R2754

In a DESCRIPTION, the value of the name attribute on a `soapbind:fault` element MUST match the value of the name attribute on its parent `wsdl:fault` element.

Compliant

A WSDL description generated by a .NET Web service does not contain any **wsdl:fault** or **soapbind:fault** elements.

R2722

A `wsdl:binding` in a DESCRIPTION MAY specify the `use` attribute on contained `soapbind:fault` elements.

Compliant

A WSDL description generated by a .NET Web service does not contain any **soapbind:fault** elements.

R2723

If in a `wsdl:binding` in a DESCRIPTION the `use` attribute on a contained `soapbind:fault` element is present, its value MUST be "literal".

Compliant

A WSDL description generated by a .NET Web service does not contain any **soapbind:fault** elements.

R2728

A `wsdl:binding` in a DESCRIPTION that omits the `use` attribute on a contained `soapbind:fault` element MUST be interpreted as though `use=`"literal" had been specified.

Compliant

A WSDL description generated by a .NET Web service does not contain any **soapbind:fault** elements.

R2724

If an INSTANCE receives a message that is inconsistent with its WSDL description, it SHOULD generate a `soap:Fault` with a faultcode of "Client", unless a "MustUnderstand" or "VersionMismatch" is generated.

Compliant

This is not mandatory. A .NET Web service does not return a **soap:Fault** if the message is inconsistent with its WSDL description unless there are inconsistencies such as a method it does not recognize.

R2725

If an INSTANCE receives a message that is inconsistent with its WSDL description, it MUST check for "VersionMismatch", "MustUnderstand", and "Client" fault conditions in that order.

Unique

A .NET Web service will automatically check first for a **VersionMismatch** error when validating the incoming message. It then automatically parses the message for header and parameter values and will return a Client error if the values cannot be parsed against the expected data types. Once those two automatic steps are completed, control is given to your **Webmethod**, where you must check first for **MustUnderstand** faults (reference rule 1025 for example).

R2729

A MESSAGE described with an rpc-literal binding that is a response message MUST have a wrapper element whose name is the corresponding `wsdl:operation` name suffixed with the string "Response".

Unique

A .NET Web service does not support an rpc-literal binding.

R2735

A MESSAGE described with an rpc-literal binding MUST place the part accessor elements for parameters and return value in no namespace.

Unique

A .NET Web service does not support an rpc-literal binding.

R2737

A MESSAGE described with an rpc-literal binding MUST namespace qualify the children of part accessor elements for the parameters and the return value with the targetNamespace in which their types are defined.

Unique

A .NET Web service does not support an rpc-literal binding.

R2738

A MESSAGE MUST include all `soapbind:headers` specified on a `wsdl:input` or `wsdl:output` of a `wsdl:operation` of a `wsdl:binding` that describes it.

Typically Compliant

A .NET Web service properly handles a SOAP message that adheres to this rule. However, you must not use a **SoapHeaderAttribute** with the **Direction** property set to **SoapHeaderDirection.Fault**. This is because the WSDL description includes a **soapbind:header** element on the **wsdl:output**, but the response message does not include a **soap:header** for it.

R2739

A MESSAGE MAY contain SOAP header blocks that are not described in the `wsdl:binding` that describes it.

Compliant

A .NET Web service properly handles a SOAP message that adheres to this rule. SOAP headers that are passed in that have not been declared can be accessed by using a **SoapHeaderAttribute** with a variable declared as an array of type **SoapUnknownHeader**. Here is an example:

```
public SoapUnknownHeader[] unknownHeaders;

[WebMethod]
[SoapHeader("unknownHeaders", Required=false)]
public string HelloWorld()
{
// check the unknownHeaders array to see if any undeclared
// header blocks were passed in the SOAP message
}
```

R2753

A MESSAGE containing SOAP header blocks that are not described in the appropriate `wsdl:binding` MAY have the `mustUnderstand` attribute on such SOAP header blocks set to '1'.

Compliant

A .NET Web service properly handles a SOAP message that adheres to this rule. SOAP headers that are passed in that have not been declared can be accessed by using a **SoapHeaderAttribute** with a variable declared as an array of type **SoapUnknownHeader**. Here is an example:

```
public SoapUnknownHeader[] unknownHeaders;

[WebMethod]
[SoapHeader("unknownHeaders", Required=false)]
public string HelloWorld()
{
    // Check for unknown headers marked as mandatory
    foreach (SoapUnknownHeader header in unknownHeaders)

    {
        if (header.MustUnderstand)
        {
        // Process SOAP header marked as mustUnderstand
        }
    }
}
```

R2751

The order of `soapbind:header` elements in `soapbind:binding` sections of a DESCRIPTION MUST be considered independent of the order of SOAP header blocks in the message.

Compliant

A .NET Web service properly handles the SOAP header blocks regardless of the order.

R2752

A MESSAGE MAY contain more then one instance of each SOAP header block for each `soapbind:header` element in the appropriate child of `soapbind:binding` in the corresponding description.

Compliant

A .NET Web service properly handles a SOAP message that adheres to this rule. When you use a **SoapHeaderAttribute**, any additional instances of that header beyond the first one in the SOAP message are treated as an unknown header and can be accessed by using a **SoapHeaderAttribute** with a variable declared as an array of type **SoapUnknownHeader**.

R2744

A HTTP request MESSAGE MUST contain a `SOAPAction` HTTP header field with a quoted value equal to the value of the `soapAction` attribute of `soapbind:operation`, if present in the corresponding WSDL description.

Compliant

A .NET Web service properly handles an HTTP request message that adheres to this rule. A WSDL description generated by a .NET Web service includes a **soapAction** attribute on **soapbind:operation** elements.

R2745

A HTTP request MESSAGE MUST contain a `SOAPAction` HTTP header field with a quoted empty string value, if in the corresponding WSDL description, the `soapAction` of `soapbind:operation` is either not present, or present with an empty string as its value.

Compliant

A .NET Web service properly handles an HTTP request message that adheres to this rule. A WSDL description generated by a .NET Web service includes a **soapAction** attribute on **soapbind:operation** elements.

R2747

A CONSUMER MUST understand and process all WSDL 1.1 SOAP Binding extension elements, irrespective of the presence or absence of the `wsdl:required` attribute on an extension element; and irrespective of the value of the `wsdl:required` attribute, when present.

Not applicable

This rule is not applicable to creating a Web service. A WSDL description generated by a .NET Web service does not include **wsdl:required** attributes on WSDL 1.1 SOAP Binding extension elements.

R2748

A CONSUMER MUST NOT interpret the presence of the `wsdl:required` attribute on a `soapbind` extension element with a value of "false" to mean the extension element is optional in the messages generated from the WSDL description.

Not applicable

This rule is not applicable to creating a Web service. A WSDL description generated by a .NET Web service does not include **wsdl:required** attributes on **soapbind** extension elements.

XML Schema

An XML schema represents the interrelationship between the attributes and elements of an XML object (for example, a document or a portion of a document). To create a schema for a document, you analyze its structure, defining each structural element as you encounter it. For example, within a schema for a document describing a Web site, you would define a Web site element, a Web page element, and other elements that describe possible content divisions within any page on that site. Just as in HTML, elements are defined within a set of tags.

R2800

A DESCRIPTION MAY use any construct from XML Schema 1.0.

Compliant

A WSDL description generated by a .NET Web service adheres to this rule.

R2801

A DESCRIPTION MUST use XML Schema 1.0 Recommendation as the basis of user defined datatypes and structures.

Compliant

A WSDL description generated by a .NET Web service adheres to this rule.

Service Publication and Discovery

The purpose of a UDDI registry is to give people a way to find and use a Web service. The UDDI registry accepts information describing a business, including the Web services it offers, and allows users to perform online searches and to download information. The two main parts of UDDI are registration (or publication) and discovery. Registration means that businesses can post information to UDDI that other businesses can search for and discover. UDDI registration is contained in a variety of data structures, two of which, binding templates and tModels, are addressed in the Basic Profile.

Binding Templates

A *binding template* is a UDDI data structure that organizes information for specific instances of service types. When businesses want to make their specification-compliant services available to the registry, they include a reference to the tModelKey (see below) for that service type in their binding template data. Binding templates provide information for physically accessing a Web service that is registered with UDDI. Examples of the access points in the **bindingTemplate** structure include **mailto:**, **http:**, and **phone:**.

R3100

REGDATA of type `uddi:bindingTemplate` representing a conformant INSTANCE MUST contain the `uddi:accessPoint` element.

Not applicable

The UDDI registration of a Web service is outside the scope of creating a Web service.

tModels

In UDDI terms, a *tModel* is the mechanism used to exchange metadata about a Web service, such as the Web service description, or a pointer to a WSDL file. A tModel is a data structure representing a *service type* (a generic representation of a registered service) in the UDDI registry. Each business registered with UDDI categorizes all of its Web services according to a defined list of service types. Businesses can search the registry's listed service types to find service providers. The tModel is an abstraction for a technical specification of a service type; it organizes the service type's information and makes it accessible in the registry database. Each tModel consists of a name, an explanatory description, and a Universal Unique Identifier (UUID). The tModel *name* identifies the service, such as, for example, "online order placement." The *description* supplies more information, which in this case might be *place an order online*. The unique identifier, called a *tModelKey*, is a series of alphanumeric characters, such as, for example, uuid:4CD7E4BC-648B-426D-9936-443EAAC8AI.

Another example, the tModel uddi-org:http has the description An http or Web browser based Web service, and the tModelKey uuid:68DE9E80-AD09-469D-8A37-088422BFBC36.

R3002

REGDATA of type `uddi:tModel` representing a conformant Web service type MUST use WSDL as the description language.

Not applicable

The UDDI registration of a Web service is outside the scope of building a Web service.

R3003

REGDATA of type `uddi:tModel` representing a conformant Web service type MUST be categorized using the uddi:types taxonomy and a categorization of "wsdlSpec".

Not applicable

The UDDI registration of a Web service is outside the scope of creating a Web service.

R3010

REGDATA of type `uddi:tModel` representing a conformant Web service type MUST follow V1.08 of the UDDI Best Practice for Using WSDL in a UDDI Registry (*http://www.oasis-open.org/committees/uddi-spec/doc/bp/uddi-spec-tc-bp-using-wsdl-v108-20021110.htm*).

Not applicable

The UDDI registration of a Web service is outside the scope of creating a Web service.

R3011

The wsdl:binding that is referenced by REGDATA of type `uddi:tModel` MUST itself conform to the profile.

Not Applicable

The UDDI registration of a Web service is outside the scope of creating a Web service.

Security

For implementing Web service clients, the basic profile offers guidance on using HTTPS and on certificate authorities when invoking a Web service.

The Use of HTTPS

HTTPS tunnels HTTP messages over a secure network connection protected by the using the SSL/TLS protocol (Secure Sockets Layer/Transport Layer Security), which is commonly called SSL.

R5000

An INSTANCE MAY require the use of HTTPS.

Compliant

To require the use of HTTPS for a .NET Web service, configure IIS by setting directory security to force SSL.

R5001

If an INSTANCE requires the use of HTTPS, the location attribute of the `soapbind:address` element in its `wsdl:port` description MUST be a URI whose scheme is "https"; otherwise it MUST be a URI whose scheme is "http".

Compliant

A WSDL description generated by a .NET Web service sets the URI of the location attribute on the **soapbind:address** element to "https" if, when querying for the WSDL description, https is used. Otherwise, the URI of the location attribute is "http". By setting directory security in IIS to force SSL, you force queries for the WSDL description to use https.

R5010

An INSTANCE MAY require the use of HTTPS with mutual authentication.

Compliant

To require use of HTTPS with mutual authentication for a .NET Web service, configure IIS by setting directory security to force SSL and to require client certificates.

5

Applying Basic Profile Rules When Consuming Web Services

Developers who write Web service clients may find that they need to adjust their code to make it comply with the constraints set forth in the Basic Profile. To provide some guidance on how to make these adjustments, we first made some general assumptions about how a developer will implement a client that consumes Web services.

These assumptions are made for the purposes of this chapter because otherwise they would apply very broadly. For example, if alternatives to using **SoapHttpClientProtocol** (such as **HttpWebRequest**) were considered for each rule, then a large portion of rules would be listed as potentially compliant since using something like **HttpWebRequest** allows very flexible control in the request allowing for a violation of the rule.

These assumptions are:

- The Web client is implemented as a class derived from the .NET **SoapHttpClientProtocol** class, The Visual Studio .NET **Add Web Reference** wizard generates a template class derived from the **SoapHttpClientProtocol** class when it creates a client that consumes a Web service.
- No parameters, return values, or headers contain **XmlNode** types.
- The Web service and its WSDL description are compliant with the WS-I Basic Profile.

Next, we assigned each of the Basic Profile rules one of four possible levels of compliance. These levels indicate how closely a client written according to our assumptions complies with the rules' requirements. These levels are:

- Compliant—this means that if the profile rule is applicable to your client or the Web service you are using, you will not need to make any code changes to meet the requirements of the rule. Note that "weak" rules that contain SHOULD or MAY are classified as compliant when the Web client does not meet their requirements. This is because these rules aren't mandatory. See R2008 for an example.
- Typically compliant—this means that if the particular profile rule is applicable to your client or the Web service you are using, it probably meets the requirements of the rule but there is a possibility it needs code adjustments.
- Potentially compliant—this means that if the particular profile rule is applicable to your client or the Web service you are using, you will probably need to make code adjustments to make your Web client meet the rule's requirements.
- Unique—this means that if the profile rule is applicable to your client or the Web service you are using, you will need to make code adjustments such as using **HttpWebRequest** for more low-level control.

All directives are included in the same groups (such as messaging) and order as they are listed in the Basic Profile. Note that only the rule numbers and directives are included here. For the complete text, consult the WS-I Basic Profile at *http://www.ws-i.org/Profiles/Basic/2002-10/BasicProfile-1.0-WGD.htm*. The next entry after the rule is the level of compliancy and the final entry includes comments, suggestions and code samples. Here is an example of the format:

R0001 ← Profile rule number

An INSTANCE MUST be described by a WSDL 1.1 service description, by a UDDI binding template, or both. **← Profile rule**

Compliant ← Level of compliancy

A .NET Web service supports generating a WSDL 1.1 service description by using reflection on the **WebService** class. **← Comment**

Messaging

Messaging is the exchange of protocol elements, usually over a network. Messages encapsulate information transmitted to and from a Web service. These messages do not provide programming instructions; rather they specify to a Web services server which operations to invoke. According to the WS-I Basic Profile, the messaging system uses the following standards at the specified version levels:

- Simple Object Access Protocol (SOAP) 1.1 (*http://www.w3.org/TR/SOAP/*)
- Extensible Markup Language (XML) 1.0 (Second Edition) (*http://www.w3.org/TR/REC-xml*)
- RFC2616: Hypertext Transfer Protocol—HTTP/1.1 (*http://www.ietf.org/rfc/rfc2616*)
- RFC2965: HTTP State Management Mechanism (*http://www.ietf.org/rfc/rfc2965*)

XML Representation of SOAP Messages

This section includes directives in section 3.1 of the Basic Profile, which deals with the XML representation of SOAP messages. All these directives are based on the SOAP 1.1, Section 4 standard (*http://www.w3.org/TR/SOAP#_Toc478383494*).

R0001

An INSTANCE MUST be described by a WSDL 1.1 service description, by a UDDI binding template, or both.

Compliant

The **Add Web Reference** wizard in Visual Studio.NET supports importing a WSDL 1.1 description either directly or through a UDDI registry.

R0002

A DESCRIPTION MAY contain conformance claims regarding instances, as specified in the conformance claim schema.

Unique

The **Add Web Reference** wizard in Visual Studio.NET fails with a WSDL description that contains conformance claims. You need to manually remove the **wsi:Claim** elements to have the wizard properly process the WSDL description.

R0003

A DESCRIPTION's conformance claims MUST be children of the `wsdl:documentation` element of each of the elements: `wsdl:port`, `wsdl:binding`, `wsdl:portType`, `wsdl:operation` (as a child element of `wsdl:portType` but not of `wsdl:binding`) and `wsdl:message`.

Unique

The **Add Web Reference** wizard in Visual Studio.NET fails with a WSDL description that contains conformance claims. You need to manually remove the **wsi:Claim** elements to have the wizard properly process the WSDL description.

R0004

A MESSAGE MAY contain conformance claims, as specified in the conformance claim schema.

Compliant

When you invoke a Web service using the proxy class generated by the **Add Web Reference** wizard in Visual Studio.NET, the default is to exclude conformance claims. To include a conformance claim, you must manually modify the proxy class to include a conformance claim header, and make sure to set the header property to a valid instance of the header before invoking the Web service. The following example demonstrates how to modify the proxy class to include the conformance claim (bold lines are the necessary additional code):

```
// Existing web service class declaration
public class MyWebService : SoapHttpClientProtocol {

  // Add claim header variable declaration
  public ClaimHeaderType ClaimHeaderValue;
  // Other existing header variable declarations

  // Add claim soap header
  [SoapHeaderAttribute("ClaimHeaderValue")]
  // Existing web method declaration

}

// Add ClaimHeaderType class
[XmlRoot ("Claim",
    Namespace="http://ws-i.org/schemas/conformanceClaim/",
    IsNullable=false)]
public class ClaimHeaderType : SoapHeader
{
  [XmlAttribute ()]
  public string conformsTo = "http://ws-i.org/profiles/basic/1.0";
}
```

R0005

A MESSAGE's conformance claims MUST be carried as SOAP header blocks.

Compliant

When you invoke a Web service using the proxy class generated by the **Add Web Reference** wizard in Visual Studio.NET, the default is to exclude conformance claims.

R0006

A MESSAGE MAY contain conformance claims for more than one profile.

Compliant

When you invoke a Web service using the proxy class generated by the **Add Web Reference** wizard in Visual Studio.NET, the default is to exclude conformance claims.

R0007

A SENDER MUST NOT use the `soap:mustUnderstand` attribute when sending a SOAP header block containing a conformance claim.

Compliant

When you invoke a Web service using the proxy class generated by the **Add Web Reference** wizard in Visual Studio.NET, the default is to exclude conformance claims. If you manually modify the proxy class to include a conformance claim, do not set the **MustUnderstand** property of the **SoapHeader** to **true**.

R3020

REGDATA of type `uddi:tModel` claiming conformance with a Profile MUST be categorized using the ws-i-org:conformsTo:2002_12 taxonomy.

Not applicable

Visual Studio.NET does not provide a tool for registering a Web service in a UDDI registry.

R3030

REGDATA of type `uddi:tModel` claiming conformance with a Profile MUST use the ws-i-org:conformsTo:2002_12 categorization value corresponding to the conformance claim URI for that Profile.

Not applicable

Visual Studio.NET does not provide a tool for registering a Web service in a UDDI registry.

R3021

A REGISTRY MUST support the WS-I Conformance category system by adding the ws-i-org:conformsTo:2002_12 tModel definition in its registry content.

Not applicable

Visual Studio.NET does not provide a tool for registering a Web service in a UDDI registry.

R3005

REGDATA other than `uddi:tModel` elements representing conformant Web service types MUST NOT be categorized using the ws-i-org:conformsTo:2002_12 taxonomy and a categorization of "http://ws-i.org/profiles/basic/1.0".

Not applicable

Visual Studio.NET does not provide a tool for registering a Web service in a UDDI registry.

R3004

REGDATA of type `uddi:tModel` MUST be constructed so that the conformance claim it makes is consistent with the conformance claim made by the `wsdl:binding` to which it refers.

Not applicable

Visual Studio.NET does not provide a tool for registering a Web service in a UDDI registry.

R4001

A RECEIVER MUST accept messages that include the Unicode Byte Order Mark (BOM).

Not applicable

This rule is not applicable to consuming a Web service. When you invoke a Web service using the proxy class generated by the **Add Web Reference** wizard in Visual Studio.NET, the default is to exclude the BOM. The following example demonstrates how to use the **RequestEncoding** property to include the BOM in the message:

```
localhost.Service1 myService = new localhost.Service1()
// passing true to the UTF8Encoding constructor tells
// it to include the Unicode BOM
myService.RequestEncoding = new System.Text.UTF8Encoding(true);
String result = myService.HelloWorld();
```

R1000

When a MESSAGE contains a `soap:Fault` element, that element MUST NOT have element children other than `faultcode`, `faultstring`, `faultactor` and `detail`.

Compliant

When you invoke a Web service using the proxy class generated by the **Add Web Reference** wizard in Visual Studio.NET, it properly treats a returned fault message that adheres to this rule as a **SoapException**.

R1001

When a MESSAGE contains a `soap:Fault` element its element children MUST be unqualified.

Compliant

When you invoke a Web service using the proxy class generated by the **Add Web Reference** wizard in Visual Studio.NET, it properly treats a returned fault message that adheres to this rule as a **SoapException**.

R1002

A RECEIVER MUST accept fault messages that have any number of elements, including zero, appearing as children of the `detail` element. Such children can be qualified or unqualified.

Compliant

When you invoke a Web service using the proxy class generated by the **Add Web Reference** wizard in Visual Studio.NET, it properly treats a returned fault message that adheres to this rule as a **SoapException**.

R1003

A RECEIVER MUST accept fault messages that have any number of qualified or unqualified attributes, including zero, appearing on the `detail` element. The namespace of qualified attributes can be anything other than "http://schemas.xmlsoap.org/soap/envelope/".

Compliant

When you invoke a Web service using the proxy class generated by the **Add Web Reference** wizard in Visual Studio.NET, it properly treats a returned fault message that adheres to this rule as a **SoapException**.

R1016

A RECEIVER MUST accept fault messages that carry an `xml:lang` attribute on the `faultstring` element.

Compliant

When you invoke a Web service using the proxy class generated by the **Add Web Reference** wizard in Visual Studio.NET, it properly treats a returned fault message that adheres to this rule as a **SoapException**.

R1004

When a MESSAGE contains a `faultcode` element the content of that element SHOULD be one of the fault codes defined in SOAP 1.1 or a namespace qualified fault code.

Compliant

When you invoke a Web service using the proxy class generated by the **Add Web Reference** wizard in Visual Studio.NET, it properly treats a returned fault message that either does or does not adhere to this rule as a **SoapException**.

R1031

When a MESSAGE contains a faultcode element the content of that element SHOULD NOT use the SOAP 1.1 "dot" notation to refine the meaning of the Fault.

Compliant

When you invoke a Web service using the proxy class generated by the **Add Web Reference** wizard in Visual Studio.NET, it properly treats a returned fault message that either does or does not adhere to this rule as a **SoapException**

R1005

A MESSAGE MUST NOT contain `soap:encodingStyle` attributes on any of the elements whose namespace name is "http://schemas.xmlsoap.org/soap/envelope/".

Compliant

When you invoke a Web service using the proxy class generated by the **Add Web Reference** wizard in Visual Studio.NET, it generates a message that adheres to this rule. When a Web service uses either the document/encoded or rpc/encoded format, it requires **soap:encodingStyle** attributes to be included in the SOAP message. Since the Basic Profile prohibits these two formats, a proxy class generated for a conformant Web service does not generate messages that use **soap:encodingStyle** attributes.

R1006

A MESSAGE MUST NOT contain `soap:encodingStyle` attributes on any element that is a child of `soap:Body`.

Compliant

When you invoke a Web service using the proxy class generated by the **Add Web Reference** wizard in Visual Studio.NET, it generates a message that adheres to this rule.

R1007

A MESSAGE described in an rpc-literal binding MUST NOT contain `soap:encodingStyle` attribute on any elements are grandchildren of `soap:Body`.

Unique

The **Add Web Reference** wizard in Visual Studio.NET cannot process a WSDL description that uses an rpc-literal binding.

R1008

A MESSAGE MUST NOT contain a Document Type Declaration.

Compliant

When you invoke a Web service using the proxy class generated by the **Add Web Reference** wizard in Visual Studio.NET, it generates a message that adheres to this rule.

R1009

A MESSAGE MUST NOT contain Processing Instructions.

Compliant

When you invoke a Web service using the proxy class generated by the **Add Web Reference** wizard in Visual Studio.NET, it generates a message that adheres to this rule.

R1010

A RECEIVER MUST accept messages that contain an XML Declaration.

Compliant

When you invoke a Web service using the proxy class generated by the **Add Web Reference** wizard in Visual Studio.NET, it always generates the **XML Declaration** on the message and properly handles a response message that adheres to this rule.

R1011

A MESSAGE MUST NOT have any element children of `soap:Envelope` following the `soap:Body` element.

Compliant

When you invoke a Web service using the proxy class generated by the **Add Web Reference** wizard in Visual Studio.NET, it generates a message that adheres to this rule.

R1012

A MESSAGE MUST be serialized as either UTF-8 or UTF-16.

Typically Compliant

When you invoke a Web service using the proxy class generated by the **Add Web Reference** wizard in Visual Studio.NET, it will, by default, use UTF-8 encoding. You can specify what encoding to use by setting the **RequestEncoding** property. In this case, you must use either UnicodeEncoding or UTF8Encoding. The following example shows how to specify UTF-16 encoding (Unicode):

```
localhost.Service1 myService = new localhost.Service1();
// Sets the encoding style to use UTF-16
myService.RequestEncoding = System.Text.Encoding.Unicode;
String result = myService.HelloWorld();
```

R1018

The media type of a MESSAGE's envelope MUST indicate the correct character encoding, using the charset parameter.

Compliant

When you invoke a Web service using the proxy class generated by the **Add Web Reference** wizard in Visual Studio.NET, it generates a message that adheres to this rule.

R1013

A MESSAGE containing a `soap:mustUnderstand` attribute MUST only use the lexical forms "0" and "1".

Compliant

When you invoke a Web service using the proxy class generated by the **Add Web Reference** wizard in Visual Studio.NET, it generates a message that adheres to this rule. If any of the methods of the Web service have headers defined, a property will exist in the proxy class for each header. The property type will be a class inherited from **SoapHeader**, which has a **MustUnderstand** property. Depending on the value of the **MustUnderstand** property for each header, the proxy class will generate a **soap:mustUnderstand** attribute with the value of either "0" or "1".

R1014

The children of the `soap:Body` element in a MESSAGE MUST be namespace qualified.

Compliant

When you invoke a Web service using the proxy class generated by the **Add Web Reference** wizard in Visual Studio.NET, it generates a message that adheres to this rule.

R1015

A RECEIVER MUST generate a fault if they encounter a message whose document element has a local name of "Envelope" but a namespace name that is not "http://schemas.xmlsoap.org/soap/envelope/".

Compliant

When you invoke a Web service using the proxy class generated by the **Add Web Reference** wizard in Visual Studio.NET, it generates a message that adheres to this rule.

R1017

A RECEIVER MUST NOT mandate the use of the `xsi:type` attribute in messages except as required in order to indicate a derived type (see XML Schema Part 1: Structures, Section 2.6.1).

Compliant

When you invoke a Web service using the proxy class generated by the **Add Web Reference** wizard in Visual Studio.NET, it will properly handle a response message that adheres to this rule.

The Soap Processing Model

This portion includes directives in section 3.2 of the Basic Profile, which alludes to information in SOAP 1.1, Section 2 (*http://www.w3.org/TR/SOAP#_Toc478383491*). SOAP 1.1, Section 2 defines a model for processing messages.

R1025

A RECEIVER MUST handle messages in such a way that it appears that all checking of mandatory headers is performed before any actual processing.

Not Applicable

This rule is not applicable to consuming a Web service.

R1027

A RECEIVER MUST generate a "soap:MustUnderstand" fault when a message contains a mandatory header block (i.e., one that has a `soap:mustUnderstand` attribute with the value "1") targeted at the receiver (via `soap:actor`) that the receiver does not understand.

Not Applicable

This rule is not applicable to consuming a Web service.

R1028

When a Fault is generated by a RECEIVER, further processing SHOULD NOT be performed on the SOAP message aside from that which is necessary to rollback, or compensate for, any effects of processing the message prior to the generation of the Fault.

Not Applicable

This rule is not applicable to consuming a Web service.

R1029

Where the normal outcome of processing a SOAP message would have resulted in the transmission of a SOAP response, but rather a SOAP Fault is generated instead, a RECEIVER MUST transmit a SOAP Fault message in place of the response.

Not Applicable

This rule is not applicable to consuming a Web service.

R1030

A RECEIVER that generates a SOAP Fault SHOULD notify the end user that a SOAP Fault has been generated when practical, by whatever means is deemed appropriate to the circumstance.

Compliant

Although it is not mandatory, when you invoke a Web service using the proxy class generated by the **Add Web Reference** wizard in Visual Studio.NET, the end user should be notified of a fault if a **SoapException** is returned.

Using SOAP in HTTP

This portion includes directives in section 3.3 of the Basic Profile, which alludes to information in the following specifications:

- SOAP 1.1, Section 6 (*http://www.w3.org/TR/SOAP/#_Toc478383526*)
- HTTP/1.1 (*http://www.ietf.org/rfc/rfc2616*)
- HTTP State Management Mechanism (*http://www.ietf.org/rfc/rfc2965*)

SOAP 1.1 defines a single protocol binding, which is for HTTP and the profile mandates the use of that binding.

HTTP/1.1 has several performance advantages and is more clearly specified in comparison to HTTP/1.0. Note that support for HTTP/1.0 is implied in HTTP/1.1, and that intermediaries may change the version of a message; for more information about HTTP versioning, see RFC2145.

R1140

A MESSAGE SHOULD be sent using HTTP/1.1.

Compliant

Although it is not mandatory, when you invoke a Web service using the proxy class generated by the **Add Web Reference** wizard in Visual Studio.NET, it sends the message using HTTP/1.1.

R1141

A MESSAGE MUST be sent using either HTTP/1.1 or HTTP/1.0.

Compliant

When you invoke a Web service using the proxy class generated by the **Add Web Reference** wizard in Visual Studio.NET, it sends the message using HTTP/1.1.

R1107

A RECEIVER MUST interpret SOAP messages containing only a `soap:Fault` element as a Fault.

Compliant

When you invoke a Web service using the proxy class generated by the **Add Web Reference** wizard in Visual Studio.NET, if the Web service response contains a **soap:Fault** element, the proxy returns a **SoapException** regardless of the HTTP status code.

R1132

A HTTP request MESSAGE MUST use the HTTP POST method.

Compliant

When you invoke a Web service using the proxy class generated by the **Add Web Reference** wizard in Visual Studio.NET, it generates a message that adheres to this rule.

R1108

A MESSAGE MUST NOT use the HTTP Extension Framework (RFC2774).

Compliant

When you invoke a Web service using the proxy class generated by the **Add Web Reference** wizard in Visual Studio.NET, it generates a message that adheres to this rule.

R1109

The value of the `SOAPAction` HTTP header field in a HTTP request MESSAGE MUST be a quoted string.

Compliant

When you invoke a Web service using the proxy class generated by the **Add Web Reference** wizard in Visual Studio.NET, it generates a message that adheres to this rule.

R1119

A RECEIVER MAY respond with a Fault if the value of the `SOAPAction` HTTP header field is not quoted.

Not Applicable

This rule is not applicable to consuming a Web service. When you invoke a Web service using the proxy class generated by the **Add Web Reference** wizard in Visual Studio.NET, it always makes the **SOAPAction** HTTP header field a quoted string.

R1110

An INSTANCE MAY accept connections on TCP port 80 (HTTP).

Compliant

When you invoke a Web service using the proxy class generated by the **Add Web Reference** wizard in Visual Studio.NET, it uses whichever TCP port was specified in the **location** attribute of the **soap:address** element from the WSDL description.

R1124

An INSTANCE MUST use a 2xx HTTP status code for responses that indicate a successful outcome of a request.

Compliant

When you invoke a Web service using the proxy class generated by the **Add Web Reference** wizard in Visual Studio.NET, it properly processes a response that adheres to this rule.

R1111

An INSTANCE SHOULD use a "200 OK" HTTP status code for responses that contain a SOAP message that is not a SOAP fault.

Compliant

When you invoke a Web service using the proxy class generated by the **Add Web Reference** wizard in Visual Studio.NET, it properly processes a response that either does or does not adhere to this rule.

R1112

An INSTANCE SHOULD use either a "200 OK" or "202 Accepted" HTTP status code for a response that does do not contain a SOAP message but indicates successful HTTP outcome of a request.

Compliant

When you invoke a Web service using the proxy class generated by the **Add Web Reference** wizard in Visual Studio.NET, it properly processes a response that adheres to this rule.

R1130

An INSTANCE MUST use HTTP status code "307 Temporary Redirect" when redirecting a request to a different endpoint.

Not Applicable

This rule is not applicable to consuming a Web service. When you invoke a Web service using the proxy class generated by the **Add Web Reference** wizard in Visual Studio.NET, it will treat a "307 Temporary Redirect" HTTP status code as an exception, allowing for the code to respond as needed.

R1131

A CONSUMER MAY automatically redirect a request when it encounters a "307 Temporary Redirect" HTTP status code in a response.

Compliant

When you invoke a Web service using the proxy class generated by the **Add Web Reference** wizard in Visual Studio.NET, it does not automatically redirect a request when it receives a "307 Temporary Redirect" HTTP status code. The following example shows how you can follow the redirect URL:

```
localhost.Service1 myService = new localhost.Service1();
string result;
bool redirect;
do
{
  redirect = false;
  try
  {
    result = myService.HelloWorld();
  }
  catch (WebException ex)
  {
    HttpWebResponse response = (HttpWebResponse)ex.Response;
    if (response.StatusCode == HttpStatusCode.TemporaryRedirect)
    {
      myService.Url = response.Headers["location"];
      redirect = true;
    }
    else
    {
      throw;
    }
  }
}
while (redirect == true);
```

R1125

An INSTANCE MUST use a 4xx HTTP status code for responses that indicate a problem with the format of the request.

Compliant

When you invoke a Web service using the proxy class generated by the **Add Web Reference** wizard in Visual Studio.NET, it properly processes a response that adheres to this rule.

R1113

An INSTANCE SHOULD use a "400 Bad Request" HTTP status code, if the request message is a malformed HTTP request, or not well-formed XML.

Compliant

When you invoke a Web service using the proxy class generated by the **Add Web Reference** wizard in Visual Studio.NET, it properly processes a response that adheres to this rule. The proxy class always generates a properly formed HTTP request containing well-formed XML.

R1114

An INSTANCE SHOULD use a "405 Method not Allowed" HTTP status code if the request method was not "POST".

Compliant

When you invoke a Web service using the proxy class generated by the **Add Web Reference** wizard in Visual Studio.NET, it properly processes a response that adheres to this rule. The proxy class always generates a request using an HTTP **POST** request method.

R1115

An INSTANCE SHOULD use a "415 Unsupported Media Type" HTTP status code if the Content-Type HTTP request header did not have a value consistent with the value specified for the corresponding binding of the input message.

Compliant

When you invoke a Web service using the proxy class generated by the **Add Web Reference** wizard in Visual Studio.NET, it properly processes a response that adheres to this rule. The proxy class always generates a request with the **Content-Type** HTTP request header set to "text/xml".

R1126

An INSTANCE MUST use a "500 Internal Server Error" HTTP status code if the response message is a SOAP Fault.

Compliant

When you invoke a Web service using the proxy class generated by the **Add Web Reference** wizard in Visual Studio.NET, it properly processes a response that adheres to this rule.

R1120

An INSTANCE MAY use the HTTP state mechanism ("Cookies").

Compliant

When you invoke a Web service using the proxy class generated by the **Add Web Reference** wizard in Visual Studio.NET, you can use the **CookieContainer** property to either send cookies or access returned cookies.

R1122

An INSTANCE using Cookies SHOULD conform to RFC2965.

Compliant

When you invoke a Web service using the proxy class generated by the **Add Web Reference** wizard in Visual Studio.NET, it properly handles a response that adheres to this rule.

R1121

An INSTANCE SHOULD NOT require consumer support for Cookies in order to function correctly.

Not applicable

This rule is not applicable to consuming a Web service.

R1123

The value of the cookie MUST be considered to be opaque by the CONSUMER.

Typically Compliant

When you invoke a Web service using the proxy class generated by the **Add Web Reference** wizard in Visual Studio.NET, you must not use the **CookieContainer** property to access cookies returned from the Web service for any purpose other then passing them back to the Web service in additional calls.

Service Description

This portion includes directives in section 4 of the Basic Profile, which alludes to information in the following specifications:

- WSDL 1.1 (*http://www.w3.org/TR/wsdl.html*)
- XML Schema Part 1: Structures (*http://www.w3.org/TR/xmlschema-1*)
- XML Schema Part 2: Datatypes (*http://www.w3.org/TR/xmlschema-2*)

The WSDL specification describes and publishes the formats and protocols of a Web service in a standard way. WSDL elements contain a description of the data, usually in XML, that is passed to the Web service so that both the sender and the receiver understand the data being exchanged. The WSDL elements also contain a description of the operations to be performed on that data so that the receiver of the message knows how to process it, and a binding to a protocol or a transport, so that the sender knows how to send it. Typically, WSDL is used with SOAP, and the WSDL specification includes a SOAP binding.

XML provides the description, storage, and transmission format for data exchanged via a Web service. XML elements and attributes define type and structure information for the data they carry. The XML syntax specifies how data is generically represented, defines how and with what qualities of service the data is transmitted, and details how the services are published and discovered.

Document Structure

This portion includes directives in section 4.2 of the Basic Profile, which alludes to information in WSDL 1.1 (*http://www.w3.org/TR/wsdl.html*) This defines an XML-based structure for describing Web services.

R2028

A DESCRIPTION using the WSDL namespace (prefixed "wsdl" in this Profile) MUST be valid according to the XML Schema found at "http://schemas.xmlsoap.org/wsdl/2003-02-11.xsd".

Compliant

The **Add Web Reference** wizard in Visual Studio.NET properly processes a WSDL description that adheres to this rule.

R2029

A DESCRIPTION using the WSDL SOAP binding namespace (prefixed "soapbind" in this Profile) MUST be valid according to the XML Schema found at "http://schemas.xmlsoap.org/wsdl/soap/2003-02-11.xsd".

Compliant

The **Add Web Reference** wizard in Visual Studio.NET properly processes a WSDL description that adheres to this rule.

R2001

A DESCRIPTION MUST only use the WSDL "import" statement to import another WSDL description.

Compliant

The **Add Web Reference** wizard in Visual Studio.NET properly processes a WSDL description that adheres to this rule.

R2002

To import XML Schema Definitions, a DESCRIPTION MUST use the XML Schema "import" statement.

Compliant

The **Add Web Reference** wizard in Visual Studio.NET properly processes a WSDL description that adheres to this rule.

R2003

A DESCRIPTION MUST use the XML Schema "import" statement only within the `xsd:schema` element of the types section.

Compliant

The **Add Web Reference** wizard in Visual Studio.NET properly processes a WSDL description that adheres to this rule.

R2004

A DESCRIPTION MUST NOT use the XML Schema "import" statement to import a Schema from any document whose root element is not "schema" from the namespace "http://www.w3.org/2001/XMLSchema".

Compliant

The **Add Web Reference** wizard in Visual Studio.NET properly processes a WSDL description that adheres to this rule.

R2009

An XML Schema directly or indirectly imported by a DESCRIPTION MAY include the Unicode Byte Order Mark (BOM).

Compliant

The **Add Web Reference** wizard in Visual Studio.NET properly processes a WSDL description that imports an XML Schema which either does or does not include the BOM.

R2010

An XML Schema directly or indirectly imported by a DESCRIPTION MUST use either UTF-8 or UTF-16 encoding.

Compliant

The **Add Web Reference** wizard in Visual Studio.NET properly processes a WSDL description that imports an XML Schema in either UTF-8 or UTF-16 encoding format.

R2011

An XML Schema directly or indirectly imported by a DESCRIPTION MUST use version 1.0 of the eXtensible Markup Language W3C Recommendation.

Compliant

The **Add Web Reference** wizard in Visual Studio.NET properly processes a WSDL description that adheres to this rule.

R2007

A DESCRIPTION MUST specify a non-empty location attribute on the `wsdl:import` element.

Compliant

The **Add Web Reference** wizard in Visual Studio.NET properly processes a WSDL description that adheres to this rule.

R2008

In a DESCRIPTION the value of the location attribute of a `wsdl:import` element SHOULD be treated as a hint.

Compliant

This is not mandatory.The **Add Web Reference** wizard in Visual Studio.NET always attempts to download the WSDL description specified with the **location** attribute.

R2022

When they appear in a DESCRIPTION, `wsdl:import` elements MUST precede all other elements from the WSDL namespace except `wsdl:documentation`.

Compliant

The **Add Web Reference** wizard in Visual Studio.NET properly processes a WSDL description that adheres to this rule.

R2023

When they appear in a DESCRIPTION, `wsdl:types` elements MUST precede all other elements from the WSDL namespace except `wsdl:documentation` and `wsdl:import`.

Compliant

The **Add Web Reference** wizard in Visual Studio.NET properly processes a WSDL description that adheres to this rule.

R4004

A DESCRIPTION MUST use version 1.0 of the eXtensible Markup Language W3C Recommendation.

Compliant

The **Add Web Reference** wizard in Visual Studio.NET properly processes a WSDL description that adheres to this rule.

R4002

A DESCRIPTION MAY include the Unicode Byte Order Mark (BOM).

Compliant

The **Add Web Reference** wizard in Visual Studio.NET properly processes a WSDL description that either includes or does not include a BOM.

R4003

A DESCRIPTION MUST use either UTF-8 or UTF-16 encoding.

Typically Compliant

The **Add Web Reference** wizard in Visual Studio.NET properly processes a WSDL description that uses UTF-8 encoding, but cannot process one using UTF-16 encoding.

R2005

The `targetNamespace` attribute on the `wsdl:definitions` element of a description that is being imported MUST have same the value as the `namespace` attribute on the `wsdl:import` element in the importing DESCRIPTION.

Compliant

The **Add Web Reference** wizard in Visual Studio.NET properly processes a WSDL description that adheres to this rule.

R2020

The `wsdl:documentation` element MAY occur as a child of the `wsdl:import` element in a DESCRIPTION.

Compliant

The **Add Web Reference** wizard in Visual Studio.NET properly processes a WSDL description that adheres to this rule.

R2021

The `wsdl:documentation` element MAY occur as a child of the `wsdl:part` element in a DESCRIPTION.

Compliant

The **Add Web Reference** wizard in Visual Studio.NET properly processes a WSDL description that adheres to this rule.

R2024

The `wsdl:documentation` element MAY occur as a first child of the `wsdl:definitions` element in a DESCRIPTION.

Compliant

The **Add Web Reference** wizard in Visual Studio.NET properly processes a WSDL description that adheres to this rule.

R2025

A DESCRIPTION containing WSDL extensions MUST NOT use them to contradict other requirements of the Profile.

Compliant

The **Add Web Reference** wizard in Visual Studio.NET properly processes a WSDL description that adheres to this rule.

R2026

A DESCRIPTION SHOULD NOT include extension elements with a `wsdl:required` attribute value of "true" on any WSDL construct (`wsdl:binding`, `wsdl:portType`, `wsdl:message`, `wsdl:types`, or `wsdl:import`) that claims conformance to the Profile.

Compliant

The **Add Web Reference** wizard in Visual Studio.NET properly processes a WSDL description that adheres to this rule.

R2027

If during the processing of an element in the WSDL namespace in a description, a consumer encounters a WSDL extension element amongst its element children, that has a `wsdl:required` attribute with a boolean value of "true" that the consumer does not understand or cannot process, the CONSUMER MUST fail processing of that element in the WSDL namespace.

Unique

The **Add Web Reference** wizard in Visual Studio.NET ignores WSDL extension elements it does not understand regardless of the **wsdl:required** attribute value, when it is present.

Types

This portion of the profile modifies and refers to WSDL 1.1, Section 2.2 (*http://www.w3.org/TR/wsdl#_types*), which describes WSDL data types.

R2101

A DESCRIPTION MUST NOT use QName references to elements in namespaces that have been neither imported, nor defined in the referring WSDL document.

Compliant

The **Add Web Reference** wizard in Visual Studio.NET properly processes a WSDL description that adheres to this rule.

R2102

A QName reference to a Schema component in a DESCRIPTION MUST use the namespace defined in the `targetNamespace` attribute on the `xsd:schema` element, or to a namespace defined in the `namespace` attribute on an `xsd:import` element within the `xsd:schema` element.

Compliant

The **Add Web Reference** wizard in Visual Studio.NET properly processes a WSDL description that adheres to this rule.

R2105

All `xsd:schema` elements contained in a `wsdl:types` element of a DESCRIPTION MUST have a `targetNamespace` attribute with a valid and non-null value, UNLESS the `xsd:schema` element has `xsd:import` and/or `xsd:annotation` as its only child element(s).

Compliant

The **Add Web Reference** wizard in Visual Studio.NET properly processes a WSDL description that adheres to this rule.

R2110

In a DESCRIPTION, `array` declarations MUST NOT extend or restrict the `soapenc:Array` type.

Compliant

The **Add Web Reference** wizard in Visual Studio.NET properly processes a WSDL description that adheres to this rule.

R2111

In a DESCRIPTION, `array` declarations MUST NOT use `wsdl:arrayType` attribute in the type declaration.

Compliant

The **Add Web Reference** wizard in Visual Studio.NET properly processes a WSDL description that adheres to this rule.

R2112

In a DESCRIPTION, `array` declaration wrapper elements SHOULD NOT be named using the convention ArrayOfXXX.

Compliant

The **Add Web Reference** wizard in Visual Studio.NET properly processes a WSDL description that adheres to this rule.

R2113

A MESSAGE containing serialized arrays MUST NOT include the `soapenc:arrayType` attribute.

Compliant

When you invoke a Web service using the proxy class generated by the **Add Web Reference** wizard in Visual Studio.NET, it generates a message that adheres to this rule.

R2114

The target namespace for WSDL definitions and the target namespace for schema definitions in a DESCRIPTION MAY be the same.

Compliant

The **Add Web Reference** wizard in Visual Studio.NET properly processes a WSDL description that adheres to this rule.

Messages

This portion of the profile modifies and refers to WSDL 1.1, Section 2.3 (*http://www.w3.org/TR/wsdl#_messages*), which describes WSDL messages.

R2201

A document-literal binding in a DESCRIPTION MUST, in each of its `soapbind:body` element(s), have at most one part listed in the `parts` attribute, if the `parts` attribute is specified.

Compliant

The **Add Web Reference** wizard in Visual Studio.NET properly processes a WSDL description that adheres to this rule.

R2210

If a document-literal binding in a DESCRIPTION does not specify the `parts` attribute on a `soapbind:body` element, the corresponding abstract `wsdl:message` MUST define zero or one `wsdl:parts`.

Compliant

The **Add Web Reference** wizard in Visual Studio.NET properly processes a WSDL description that adheres to this rule.

R2202

A `wsdl:binding` in a DESCRIPTION MAY contain `soapbind:body` element(s) that specify that zero parts form the `soap:body`.

Compliant

The **Add Web Reference** wizard in Visual Studio.NET properly processes a WSDL description that adheres to this rule.

R2203

An rpc-literal binding in a DESCRIPTION MUST refer, in its `soapbind:body` element(s), only to `wsdl:part` element(s) that have been defined using the `type` attribute.

Unique

The **Add Web Reference** wizard in Visual Studio.NET cannot process a WSDL description that uses an rpc-literal binding.

R2211

A MESSAGE described with an rpc-literal binding MUST NOT have the `xsi:nil` attribute with a value of "1" or "true" on the part accessors.

Unique

The **Add Web Reference** wizard in Visual Studio.NET cannot process a WSDL description that uses an rpc-literal binding.

R2207

A `wsdl:message` in a DESCRIPTION MAY contain `wsdl:parts` that use the `elements` attribute provided those `wsdl:parts` are not referred to by a `soapbind:body` in an rpc-literal binding.

Compliant

The **Add Web Reference** wizard in Visual Studio.NET properly processes a WSDL description that adheres to this rule.

R2204

A document-literal binding in a DESCRIPTION MUST refer, in each of its `soapbind:body` element(s), only to `wsdl:part` element(s) that have been defined using the `element` attribute.

Compliant

The **Add Web Reference** wizard in Visual Studio.NET properly processes a WSDL description that adheres to this rule.

R2208

A binding in a DESCRIPTION MAY contain `soapbind:header` element(s) that refer to `wsdl:parts` in the same `wsdl:message` that are referred to by its `soapbind:body` element(s).

Compliant

The **Add Web Reference** wizard in Visual Studio.NET properly processes a WSDL description that adheres to this rule.

R2205

A `wsdl:binding` in a DESCRIPTION MUST refer, in each of its `soapbind:header`, `soapbind:headerfault` and `soapbind:fault` elements, only to `wsdl:part` element(s) that have been defined using the `element` attribute.

Compliant

The **Add Web Reference** wizard in Visual Studio.NET properly processes a WSDL description that adheres to this rule.

R2209

A `wsdl:binding` in a DESCRIPTION SHOULD bind every `wsdl:part` of a `wsdl:message` in the `wsdl:portType` to which it refers to one of `soapbind:body`, `soapbind:header`, `soapbind:fault` or `soapbind:headerfault`.

Compliant

The **Add Web Reference** wizard in Visual Studio.NET properly processes a WSDL description that adheres to this rule.

R2206

A `wsdl:message` in a DESCRIPTION containing a `wsdl:part` that uses the `element` attribute MUST refer, in that attribute, to a global element declaration.

Compliant

The **Add Web Reference** wizard in Visual Studio.NET properly processes a WSDL description that adheres to this rule.

Port Types

A WSDL port type is an abstract set of operations mapped to one or more end points, defining the collection of operations for a binding; the collection of operations, because it is abstract, can be mapped to multiple transports through various bindings.

R2301

The order of the elements in the `soap:body` of a MESSAGE MUST be the same as that of the `wsdl:parts` in the `wsdl:message` that describes it.

Compliant

When you invoke a Web service using the proxy class generated by the **Add Web Reference** wizard in Visual Studio.NET, it generates a message that adheres to this rule. For a document-literal binding, the Basic Profile requires the **soap:body** to contain only one **wsdl:part**, and the **Add Web Reference** wizard does not support rpc-literal bindings.

R2302

A DESCRIPTION MAY use the `parameterOrder` attribute of an `wsdl:operation` element to indicate the return value and method signatures as a hint to code generators.

Compliant

The **Add Web Reference** wizard in Visual Studio.NET properly processes a WSDL description that adheres to this rule.

R2303

A DESCRIPTION MUST NOT use Solicit-Response and Notification type operations in a `wsdl:portType` definition.

Compliant

The **Add Web Reference** wizard in Visual Studio.NET properly processes a WSDL description that adheres to this rule.

R2304

A `wsdl:portType` in a DESCRIPTION MUST have operations with distinct values for their `name` attributes.

Compliant

The **Add Web Reference** wizard in Visual Studio.NET properly processes a WSDL description that adheres to this rule.

R2305

A `wsdl:portType` in a DESCRIPTION MUST be constructed so that the `parameterOrder` attribute, if present, omits at most 1 `wsdl:part` from the output message.

Compliant

The **Add Web Reference** wizard in Visual Studio.NET properly processes a WSDL description that adheres to this rule.

R2306

A `wsdl:message` in a DESCRIPTION MUST NOT specify both `type` and `element` attributes on the same `wsdl:part`.

Compliant

The **Add Web Reference** wizard in Visual Studio.NET properly processes a WSDL description that adheres to this rule.

Bindings

A WSDL binding is the concrete protocol and data formats for the operations and messages defined for a particular port type.

R2401

A `wsdl:binding` element in a DESCRIPTION MUST use WSDL SOAP Binding as defined in WSDL 1.1 Section 3.

Compliant

The **Add Web Reference** wizard in Visual Studio.NET properly processes a WSDL description that adheres to this rule.

SOAP Binding

SOAP is the most popular transport for WSDL. The SOAP specification contains predefined rules for physically representing such data types as Booleans, integers, and arrays. Binding to SOAP therefore requires the abstract data types, messages, and operations to be bound to concrete physical representations on the wire.

R2701

The `wsdl:binding` element in a DESCRIPTION MUST be constructed so that its `soapbind:binding` child element specifies the `transport` attribute.

Compliant

The **Add Web Reference** wizard in Visual Studio.NET properly processes a WSDL description that adheres to this rule.

R2702

A `wsdl:binding` in a DESCRIPTION MUST specify the HTTP transport protocol with SOAP binding. Specifically, the `transport` attribute of is `soapbind:binding` child MUST have the value "http://schemas.xmlsoap.org/soap/http".

Compliant

The **Add Web Reference** wizard in Visual Studio.NET properly processes a WSDL description that adheres to this rule.

R2705

A `wsdl:binding` in a DESCRIPTION MUST use either be a rpc-literal binding or a document-literal binding.

Typically Compliant

The **Add Web Reference** wizard in Visual Studio.NET properly processes a WSDL description that adheres to this rule if the **style** attribute value is "document." It does not support descriptions with a **style** attribute value of "rpc" and a **use** attribute value of "literal".

R2706

A `wsdl:binding` in a DESCRIPTION MUST use the value of "literal" for the `use` attribute in all `soapbind:body`, `soapbind:fault`, `soapbind:header`, and `soapbind:headerfault` elements.

Compliant

The **Add Web Reference** wizard in Visual Studio.NET properly processes a WSDL description that adheres to this rule.

R2707

A `wsdl:binding` in a DESCRIPTION that contains one or more `soapbind:body`, `soapbind:fault`, `soapbind:header`, or `soapbind:headerfault` elements that do not specify the `use` attribute MUST be interpreted as though the value "literal" had been specified in each case.

Compliant

The **Add Web Reference** wizard in Visual Studio.NET properly interprets a WSDL description in a manner that adheres to this rule.

R2709

A `wsdl:portType` in a DESCRIPTION MAY have zero or more `wsdl:bindings` that refer to it, defined in the same or other WSDL documents.

Compliant

The **Add Web Reference** wizard in Visual Studio.NET properly processes a WSDL description that adheres to this rule.

R2710

The operations in a `wsdl:binding` in a DESCRIPTION MUST result in wire signatures that are different from one another.

Compliant

The **Add Web Reference** wizard in Visual Studio.NET properly processes a WSDL description that adheres to this rule.

R2711

A DESCRIPTION SHOULD NOT have more than one `wsdl:port` with the same value for the `location` attribute of the `soapbind:address` element.

Compliant

The **Add Web Reference** wizard in Visual Studio.NET properly processes a WSDL description that adheres to this rule.

R2712

A document-literal binding MUST be represented on the wire as a MESSAGE with a `soap:Body` whose child element is an instance of the global element declaration referenced by the corresponding `wsdl:message part`.

Compliant

When you invoke a Web service using the proxy class generated by the **Add Web Reference** wizard in Visual Studio.NET, it generates a message that adheres to this rule.

R2714

For one-way operations, an INSTANCE MUST NOT return a HTTP response that contains a SOAP envelope. Specifically, the HTTP response entity-body must be empty.

Compliant

When you invoke a Web service using the proxy class generated by the **Add Web Reference** wizard in Visual Studio.NET, it properly handles a response that adheres to this rule.

R2750

A CONSUMER MUST ignore SOAP response carried in a response from a one-way operation.

Unique

When you invoke a Web service using the proxy class generated by the **Add Web Reference** wizard in Visual Studio.NET, it will read the response if it receives a 5xx HTTP response code.

R2727

For one-way operations, a CONSUMER MUST NOT interpret a successful HTTP response status code (i.e., 2xx) to mean the message is valid or that the receiver would process it.

Typically Compliant

Your client application shouldn't assume that, even if a one-way operation is successfully delivered, the message is valid or will be processed.

R2716

A document-literal binding in a DESCRIPTION MUST NOT have the `namespace` attribute specified on contained `soapbind:body`, `soapbind:header`, `soapbind:headerfault` and `soapbind:fault` elements.

Compliant

The **Add Web Reference** wizard in Visual Studio.NET properly processes a WSDL description that adheres to this rule.

R2717

An rpc-literal binding in a DESCRIPTION MUST have the `namespace` attribute specified, the value of which MUST be an absolute URI, on contained `soapbind:body` elements.

Unique

The **Add Web Reference** wizard in Visual Studio.NET cannot process a WSDL description that uses an rpc-literal binding.

R2726

An rpc-literal binding in a DESCRIPTION MUST NOT have the `namespace` attribute specified on contained `soapbind:header`, `soapbind:headerfault` and `soapbind:fault` elements.

Unique

The **Add Web Reference** wizard in Visual Studio.NET cannot process a WSDL description that uses an rpc-literal binding.

R2718

A `wsdl:binding` in a DESCRIPTION MUST have the same set of `wsdl:operations` as the `wsdl:portType` to which it refers.

Compliant

The **Add Web Reference** wizard in Visual Studio.NET properly processes a WSDL description that adheres to this rule.

R2719

A `wsdl:binding` in a DESCRIPTION MAY contain no `soapbind:headerfault` elements if there are no known header faults.

Compliant

The **Add Web Reference** wizard in Visual Studio.NET properly processes a WSDL description that adheres to this rule.

R2740

A `wsdl:binding` in a DESCRIPTION SHOULD contain a `soapbind:fault` describing each known fault.

Compliant

The **Add Web Reference** wizard in Visual Studio.NET properly processes a WSDL description that adheres to this rule.

R2741

A `wsdl:binding` in a DESCRIPTION SHOULD contain a `soapbind:headerfault` describing each known header fault.

Compliant

The **Add Web Reference** wizard in Visual Studio.NET properly processes a WSDL description that adheres to this rule.

R2742

A MESSAGE MAY contain a fault detail entry in a SOAP fault that is not described by a `wsdl:fault` element in the corresponding WSDL description.

Compliant

When you invoke a Web service using the proxy class generated by the **Add Web Reference** wizard in Visual Studio.NET, it properly handles a response that adheres to this rule.

R2743

A MESSAGE MAY contain the details of a header processing related fault in a SOAP header block that is not described by a `wsdl:headerfault` element in the corresponding WSDL description.

Compliant

When you invoke a Web service using the proxy class generated by the **Add Web Reference** wizard in Visual Studio.NET, it properly handles a response that adheres to this rule.

R2720

A `wsdl:binding` in a DESCRIPTION MUST use the attribute named `part` with a schema type of "NMTOKEN" on all contained `soapbind:header` and `soapbind:headerfault` elements.

Compliant

The **Add Web Reference** wizard in Visual Studio.NET properly processes a WSDL description that adheres to this rule.

R2749

A `wsdl:binding` in a DESCRIPTION MUST NOT use the attribute named parts on contained `soapbind:header` and `soapbind:headerfault` elements.

Compliant

The **Add Web Reference** wizard in Visual Studio.NET properly processes a WSDL description that adheres to this rule.

R2721

A `wsdl:binding` in a DESCRIPTION MUST have the `name` attribute specified on all contained `soapbind:fault` elements.

Compliant

The **Add Web Reference** wizard in Visual Studio.NET properly processes a WSDL description that adheres to this rule.

R2754

In a DESCRIPTION, the value of the name attribute on a `soapbind:fault` element MUST match the value of the name attribute on its parent `wsdl:fault` element.

Compliant

The **Add Web Reference** wizard in Visual Studio.NET properly processes a WSDL description that adheres to this rule.

R2722

A `wsdl:binding` in a DESCRIPTION MAY specify the `use` attribute on contained `soapbind:fault` elements.

Compliant

The **Add Web Reference** wizard in Visual Studio.NET properly processes a WSDL description that adheres to this rule.

R2723

If in a `wsdl:binding` in a DESCRIPTION the `use` attribute on a contained `soapbind:fault` element is present, its value MUST be "literal".

Compliant

The **Add Web Reference** wizard in Visual Studio.NET properly processes a WSDL description that adheres to this rule.

R2728

A `wsdl:binding` in a DESCRIPTION that omits the `use` attribute on a contained `soapbind:fault` element MUST be interpreted as though `use`="literal" had been specified.

Compliant

The **Add Web Reference** wizard in Visual Studio.NET properly interprets a WSDL description in a manner that adheres to this rule.

R2724

If an INSTANCE receives a message that is inconsistent with its WSDL description, it SHOULD generate a `soap:Fault` with a faultcode of "Client", unless a "MustUnderstand" or "VersionMismatch" is generated.

Not Applicable

This rule is not applicable to consuming a Web service.

R2725

If an INSTANCE receives a message that is inconsistent with its WSDL description, it MUST check for "VersionMismatch", "MustUnderstand", and "Client" fault conditions in that order.

Not Applicable

This rule is not applicable to consuming a Web service.

R2729

A MESSAGE described with an rpc-literal binding that is a response message MUST have a wrapper element whose name is the corresponding `wsdl:operation` name suffixed with the string "Response".

Unique

The **Add Web Reference** wizard in Visual Studio.NET cannot process a WSDL description that uses an rpc-literal binding to create a proxy for sending messages in an rpc-literal format.

R2735

A MESSAGE described with an rpc-literal binding MUST place the part accessor elements for parameters and return value in no namespace.

Unique

The **Add Web Reference** wizard in Visual Studio.NET cannot process a WSDL description that uses an rpc-literal binding to create a proxy for sending messages in an rpc-literal format.

R2737

A MESSAGE described with an rpc-literal binding MUST namespace qualify the children of part accessor elements for the parameters and the return value with the targetNamespace in which their types are defined.

Unique

The **Add Web Reference** wizard in Visual Studio.NET cannot process a WSDL description that uses an rpc-literal binding to create a proxy for sending messages in an rpc-literal format.

R2738

A MESSAGE MUST include all `soapbind:headers` specified on a `wsdl:input` or `wsdl:output` of a `wsdl:operation` of a `wsdl:binding` that describes it.

Potentially Compliant

The **Add Web Reference** wizard in Visual Studio.NET generates a proxy class that has a property for each **soapbind:header** specified on the **wsdl:input** of an operation. You must initialize these properties to make the SOAP message generated by the proxy class include the header.

R2739

A MESSAGE MAY contain SOAP header blocks that are not described in the `wsdl:binding` that describes it.

Unique

When you invoke a Web service using the proxy class generated by the **Add Web Reference** wizard in Visual Studio.NET, the proxy class does not support including SOAP header blocks not described in the WSDL description. To include additional SOAP header blocks, you need to modify the proxy class and add additional **SoapHeaderAttribute**s.

R2753

A MESSAGE containing SOAP header blocks that are not described in the appropriate `wsdl:binding` MAY have the `mustUnderstand` attribute on such SOAP header blocks set to '1'.

Unique

When you invoke a Web service using the proxy class generated by the **Add Web Reference** wizard in Visual Studio.NET, the proxy class does not support including SOAP header blocks not described in the WSDL description. To include additional SOAP header blocks, you need to modify the proxy class to add additional **SoapHeaderAttribute**s.

R2751

The order of `soapbind:header` elements in `soapbind:binding` sections of a DESCRIPTION MUST be considered independent of the order of SOAP header blocks in the message.

Not applicable

This rule is not applicable to consuming a Web service. When you invoke a Web service using the proxy class generated by the **Add Web Reference** wizard in Visual Studio.NET, the order of the SOAP header blocks will be in the same order as the **soapbind:header** elements of the WSDL description.

R2752

A MESSAGE MAY contain more then one instance of each SOAP header block for each `soapbind:header` element in the appropriate child of `soapbind:binding` in the corresponding description.

Unique

When you invoke a Web service using the proxy class generated by the **Add Web Reference** wizard in Visual Studio.NET, the proxy class does not support including more then one instance of a SOAP header block for a **soapbind:header** element from the WSDL description.

R2744

A HTTP request MESSAGE MUST contain a `SOAPAction` HTTP header field with a quoted value equal to the value of the `soapAction` attribute of `soapbind:operation`, if present in the corresponding WSDL description.

Compliant

When you invoke a Web service using the proxy class generated by the **Add Web Reference** wizard in Visual Studio.NET, the invocation generates a message that adheres to this rule.

R2745

A HTTP request MESSAGE MUST contain a `SOAPAction` HTTP header field with a quoted empty string value, if in the corresponding WSDL description, the `soapAction` of `soapbind:operation` is either not present, or present with an empty string as its value.

Compliant

When you invoke a Web service using the proxy class generated by the **Add Web Reference** wizard in Visual Studio.NET, the invocation generates a message that adheres to this rule.

R2747

A CONSUMER MUST understand and process all WSDL 1.1 SOAP Binding extension elements, irrespective of the presence or absence of the `wsdl:required` attribute on an extension element; and irrespective of the value of the `wsdl:required` attribute, when present.

Compliant

The **Add Web Reference** wizard in Visual Studio.NET properly interprets a WSDL description in a manner that adheres to this rule.

R2748

A CONSUMER MUST NOT interpret the presence of the `wsdl:required` attribute on a `soapbind` extension element with a value of "false" to mean the extension element is optional in the messages generated from the WSDL description.

Compliant

The **Add Web Reference** wizard in Visual Studio.NET properly interprets a WSDL description in a manner that adheres to this rule.

XML Schema

An XML schema represents the interrelationship between the attributes and elements of an XML object (for example, a document or a portion of a document). To create a schema for a document, you analyze its structure, defining each structural element as you encounter it. For example, within a schema for a document describing a Web site, you would define a Web site element, a Web page element, and other elements that describe possible content divisions within any page on that site. Just as in HTML, elements are defined within a set of tags.

R2800

A DESCRIPTION MAY use any construct from XML Schema 1.0.

Compliant

The **Add Web Reference** wizard in Visual Studio.NET properly processes a WSDL description that adheres to this rule.

R2801

A DESCRIPTION MUST use XML Schema 1.0 Recommendation as the basis of user defined datatypes and structures.

Compliant

The **Add Web Reference** wizard in Visual Studio.NET properly processes a WSDL description that adheres to this rule.

Service Publication and Discovery

The purpose of a UDDI registry is to give people a way to find and use a Web service. The UDDI registry accepts information describing a business, including the Web services it offers, and allows users to perform online searches and to download information. The two main parts of UDDI are registration (or publication) and discovery. Registration means that businesses can post information to UDDI that other businesses can search for and discover. UDDI registration is contained in a variety of data structures, two of which, binding templates and tModels, are addressed in the Basic Profile.

Binding Templates

A *binding template* is a UDDI data structure that organizes information for specific instances of service types. When businesses want to make their specification-compliant services available to the registry, they include a reference to the tModelKey (see below) for that service type in their binding template data. Binding templates provide information for physically accessing a Web service that is registered with UDDI. Examples of the access points in the **bindingTemplate** structure include **mailto:**, **http:**, and **phone:**.

R3100

REGDATA of type `uddi:bindingTemplate` representing a conformant INSTANCE MUST contain the `uddi:accessPoint` element.

Not applicable

Visual Studio.NET does not provide a tool for registering a Web service in a UDDI registry.

tModels

In UDDI terms, a *tModel* is the mechanism used to exchange metadata about a Web service, such as the Web service description, or a pointer to a WSDL file. A tModel is a data structure representing a *service type* (a generic representation of a registered service) in the UDDI registry. Each business registered with UDDI categorizes all of its Web services according to a defined list of service types. Businesses can search the registry's listed service types to find service providers. The tModel is an abstraction for a technical specification of a service type; it organizes the service type's information and makes it accessible in the registry database. Each tModel consists of a name, an explanatory description, and a Universal Unique Identifier (UUID). The tModel *name* identifies the service, such as, for example, "online order placement." The *description* supplies more information, which in this case might be *place an order online*. The unique identifier, called a *tModelKey*, is a series of alphanumeric characters, such as, for example, uuid:4CD7E4BC-648B-426D-9936-443EAAC8AI. Another example, the tModel uddi-org:http has the description An http or Web browser based Web service, and the tModelKey uuid:68DE9E80-AD09-469D-8A37-088422BFBC36.

R3002

REGDATA of type `uddi:tModel` representing a conformant Web service type MUST use WSDL as the description language.

Not applicable

Visual Studio.NET does not provide a tool for registering a Web service in a UDDI registry.

R3003

REGDATA of type `uddi:tModel` representing a conformant Web service type MUST be categorized using the uddi:types taxonomy and a categorization of "wsdlSpec".

Not applicable

Visual Studio.NET does not provide a tool for registering a Web service in a UDDI registry.

R3010

REGDATA of type `uddi:tModel` representing a conformant Web service type MUST follow V1.08 of the UDDI Best Practice for Using WSDL in a UDDI Registry (*http://www.oasis-open.org/committees/uddi-spec/doc/bp/uddi-spec-tc-bp-using-wsdl-v108-20021110.htm*).

Not applicable

Visual Studio.NET does not provide a tool for registering a Web service in a UDDI registry.

R3011

The wsdl:binding that is referenced by REGDATA of type `uddi:tModel` MUST itself conform to the profile.

Not applicable

Visual Studio.NET does not provide a tool for registering a Web service in a UDDI registry.

Security

For implementing Web service clients, the Basic Profile offers guidance on using HTTPS and on certificate authorities when invoking a Web service.

The Use of HTTPS

HTTPS tunnels HTTP messages over a secure network connection protected by the using the SSL/TLS protocol (Secure Sockets Layer/Transport Layer Security), which is commonly called SSL.

R5000

An INSTANCE MAY require the use of HTTPS.

Compliant

When you invoke a Web service using the proxy class generated by the **Add Web Reference** wizard in Visual Studio.NET, the invocation will use either HTTP or HTTPS, depending on what was specified in the **location** attribute of the **soapbind:address** element from the WSDL description.

R5001

If an INSTANCE requires the use of HTTPS, the location attribute of the `soapbind:address` element in its `wsdl:port` description MUST be a URI whose scheme is "https"; otherwise it MUST be a URI whose scheme is "http".

Compliant

When you invoke a Web service using the proxy class generated by the **Add Web Reference** wizard in Visual Studio.NET, the invocation will use either HTTP or HTTPS depending on what was specified in the **location** attribute of the **soapbind:address** element from the WSDL description.

R5010

An INSTANCE MAY require the use of HTTPS with mutual authentication.

Compliant

When you invoke a Web service using the proxy class generated by the **Add Web Reference** wizard in Visual Studio.NET, you can use the **ClientCertificates** property of the proxy class to pass a client certificate to the Web service that requires mutual authentication.

Appendix A

Appendix A groups the Basic Profile rules according to their levels of compliancy for creating Web services. Rules that do not apply to creating Web services are included in the "Not applicable" category.

Compliant

R0001
R0004
R0005
R0006
R0007
R1002
R1004
R1008
R1009
R1010
R1011
R1012
R1013
R1014
R1015
R1017
R1018
R1027
R1028
R1029
R1030
R1031
R1108
R1109
R1110
R1111
R1112
R1113
R1114
R1115
R1119
R1120
R1121
R1122
R1124
R1126
R1132
R1140
R1141
R2001
R2003
R2004
R2007
R2009
R2010
R2011
R2020
R2021
R2022
R2023
R2024
R2025
R2026
R2028
R2029
R2101
R2102
R2105
R2110
R2111
R2112
R2113
R2114
R2201
R2202
R2204
R2205
R2206
R2207
R2208
R2209
R2301
R2302
R2303
R2304
R2305
R2306
R2401
R2701
R2702
R2709
R2711
R2712
R2714
R2716
R2718
R2719
R2720
R2721
R2722
R2723
R2724
R2728
R2739
R2740
R2741
R2742
R2743
R2744
R2745
R2749
R2751
R2752
R2753
R2754
R2800
R2801
R4001
R4002
R4003
R4004
R5000
R5001
R5010

Typically Compliant

R1000
R1001
R1003
R1005
R1006
R2002
R2005
R2210
R2705
R2706
R2710
R2738

Potentially Compliant

R1025

R1130

Unique

R0002	R2203	R2729
R0003	R2211	R2735
R1007	R2717	R2737
R1016	R2725	
R1125	R2726	

Not applicable

R1107	R2707	R3002	R3011
R1123	R2727	R3003	R3020
R1131	R2747	R3004	R3021
R2008	R2748	R3005	R3030
R2027	R2750	R3010	R3100

Appendix B

Appendix B groups the Basic Profile rules according to their levels of compliancy for creating Web service clients. Rules that do not apply to creating Web service clients are included in the "Not applicable" category.

Compliant

R0001
R0004
R0005
R0006
R0007
R1000
R1001
R1002
R1003
R1004
R1005
R1006
R1008
R1009
R1010
R1011
R1013
R1014
R1015
R1016
R1017
R1018
R1030
R1031
R1107
R1108
R1109
R1110
R1111
R1112
R1113
R1114
R1115
R1120
R1122
R1124
R1125
R1126
R1131
R1132
R1140
R1141
R2001
R2002
R2003
R2004
R2005
R2007
R2008
R2009
R2010
R2011
R2020
R2021
R2022
R2023
R2024
R2025
R2026
R2028
R2029
R2101
R2102
R2105
R2110
R2111
R2112
R2113
R2114
R2201
R2202
R2204
R2205
R2206
R2207
R2208
R2209
R2210
R2301
R2302
R2303
R2304
R2305
R2306
R2401
R2701
R2702
R2706
R2707
R2709
R2710
R2711
R2712
R2714
R2716
R2718
R2719
R2720
R2721
R2722
R2723
R2728
R2740
R2741
R2742
R2743
R2744
R2745
R2747
R2748
R2749
R2754
R2800
R2801
R4002
R4004
R5000
R5001
R5010

Typically Compliant

R1012
R1123
R2705
R2727
R4003

Potentially Compliant

R2738

Unique

R0002
R0003
R1007
R2027
R2203
R2211
R2717
R2726
R2729
R2735
R2737
R2739
R2750
R2752
R2753

Not applicable

R1025
R1027
R1028
R1029
R1119
R1121
R1130
R2724
R2725
R2751
R3002
R3003
R3004
R3005
R3010
R3011
R3020
R3021
R3030
R3100
R4001

Index

S

T

U

V

W